*A Guide to Family History Resources
at the Minnesota Historical Society*

A GUIDE TO

Family History Resources

AT THE

Minnesota Historical Society

MINNESOTA HISTORICAL SOCIETY REFERENCE STAFF

MINNESOTA HISTORICAL SOCIETY PRESS

ACKNOWLEDGMENTS

This guide was produced by the following members of the Minnesota Historical Society's Reference staff: Ruth Bauer Anderson, Tracey Baker, Ron Kurpiers, Steven Nielsen, Kathryn Otto, Alison Purgiel, Alissa L. Rosenberg, Brigid Shields, Hampton Smith, Duane Swanson, Carrie M. Tannehill, and Lisa Whitehill, with the assistance of society staff members Deborah Kahn (Processing) and Deborah Swanson (Minnesota Historical Society Press).

PICTURE CREDITS

The images reproduced on the cover and in this book are from the collections of the Minnesota Historical Society, St. Paul. The name of the photographer, when known, appears in parentheses along with any other additional information.

Cover (clockwise): Man and baby, 1900–1905 (B. P. Skewis, Windom); Amelia and Basilia Diaz and Genevieve Rangel dressed as Mexican dancers for a program at Lafayette School, St. Paul, 1944 (*St. Paul Dispatch & St. Paul Pioneer Press*); the Concordia Singing Society of St. Paul picnicking about 1915; Jack, Bob, and Ralph Jones in front of 369 Jay (Galtier) St., St. Paul, 1929 (William Gardner); McGibben family orchestra, 1860–69 (Jacoby); background letter: Alexander S. Christie to Sarah J. Christie, February 19, 1865, James C. Christie and Family Papers

Page ii: A family tree: members of the Munson and Anderson families posing on the Anderson farm near Cokato about 1914 (Albert Munson)

www.mnhs.org/mhspress

The Minnesota Historical Society Press is a member of the Association of American University Presses.

Manufactured in the
United States of America

10 9 8 7 6 5 4 3 2 1

∞ The paper used in this publication meets the minimum requirements of the American National Standard for Information Sciences—Permanence for Printed Library Materials, ANSI Z39.48–1984.

International Standard Book Number
0–87351–469–6

Library of Congress
Cataloging-in-Publication Data

Minnesota Historical Society.
A guide to family history resources at the Minnesota Historical Society / Minnesota Historical Society Reference Staff.
    p.   cm.
Includes index.
ISBN 0-87351-469-6 (pbk. : alk. paper)
 1. Minnesota—Genealogy—
     Bibliography—Catalogs.
 2. Family archives—Minnesota—
     Catalogs.
 3. Minnesota Historical Society—
     Catalogs.
 I. Title.

Z1299.M67 2004
[F605]
016.929'1'0720776—dc22
2003017204

A Guide to Family History Resources at the Minnesota Historical Society

Illustrations

INTRODUCTION

THE MINNESOTA HISTORICAL SOCIETY (MHS), founded in 1849 and
the state's oldest institution, has long been recognized as the key repository for Minnesota's history. Minnesotans typically leave records of
births, marriages, and deaths, education, employment, religious and political affiliations, military service, property ownership, and relationships
to governments and the law, ranging from paying taxes and registering
a business, to living in a sanatorium or other state institution.

MHS has many of these records, as well as additional valuable items.
Besides books and other printed materials in its Library, MHS holds the
papers of prominent and not-so-prominent residents and businesses and
is a designated legal repository for most of the state's newspapers and for
the Minnesota State Archives (records documenting Minnesota government). In 1992 all of these resources were brought together in the
Minnesota History Center in St. Paul, where they are available to researchers who have discovered the value and pleasure of family history.

With the publication of *A Guide to Family History Resources at the Minnesota Historical Society*, MHS is pleased to provide an essential tool for
all genealogists who are researching Minnesota family, local, and state
history. The MHS collections are vast, and the quantity of materials for
an individual resource can range from a few pages to thousands of boxes.
The main feature of the guide is an alphabetical, annotated listing of resources by large subject areas. The materials for a resource may be partial or complete; some continue to be added to and some cover a definite
time span. The entry for each resource describes its content and may
note special restrictions, indexes, or means of access. The guide also
contains a county-by-county table of the local-government records at
MHS that are most requested by researchers. Permission is required to
obtain access to some resources, and researchers wishing to use these
resources should contact MHS for any necessary instructions or forms
before visiting in person.

The MHS Library's "Search Catalogs" web page features an on-line
catalog and is available at http://www.mnhs.org/library/search/
index.html. The on-line catalog lists books (including family, local,
county, state, and military histories), serial publications (including
newspapers, magazines, and journals), directories, indexes to passen-

ger ship lists, publications of genealogical organizations, the Minnesota State Archives records, diaries and other manuscripts, atlases and maps (including fire insurance maps), oral histories, sound recordings, videos, and other items. Also available on the web page are special indexes and research aids such as the official statewide Death Certificate Index for 1906–96 and the Visual Resources Database of photographs, portraits, and artworks (also available at http://collections.mnhs.org/visualresources). Regular researchers will want to check the on-line catalog for updates made as new resources are added to the MHS collections.

For further information, contact:
    Reference Department
    Minnesota Historical Society
    Minnesota History Center
    345 Kellogg Blvd. West
    St. Paul, MN 55102–1906
    E-mail: reference@mnhs.org
    Fax: 651-297-7436
    Telephone: 651-296-2143

Visit the MHS website at www.mnhs.org

A Guide to Family History Resources
at the Minnesota Historical Society

CENSUS RETURN OF FAMILIES

in the _____ of the _____ Tribe of Indians, residing on the lands held by the _____ and lying _____ under the 5th section of the act, approved 3d March, 1847, amending the act organizing the Indian Department. _____ Decr 21 1849

Number of families.	NAME. Of the head of each family, whether male or female, to be as it can be readily obtained.	Whole No. of the family, of all ages, and both sexes.	No. of males under the age of 18.	No. of females under the age of 16.	No. of males between the ages of 18 and 60.	No. of females between the ages of 16 and 60.	No. of males and females between the ages of 60 and 100.	No. of European or White male heads of families.	No. of European or White female heads of families.	No. of male children of half white blood.	No. of female children of half white blood.	No. of marriages in the family during the year.	No. of births, male, within the year.	No. of births, female, within the year.	No. of deaths, male, within the year.	No. of deaths, female, within the year.	No. of deaf and dumb persons in the family.	No. of lunatics or insane in the family.	No. of idiots.	No. of persons born blind.
1		1			1	1														
2		2			1	1														
3		2			1	1														
4		2			1	2														
5		3			1	2														
6		3			2	1														
7		2			1	1														
8		2			1	1														
9		2			1	1														
10		2			1	1														
11		4			1	1	1													
16		3			1															
17		4			1	1														
18		2				2														
19		3				1														
20		2																		
21		1			1	1														

Adoption Records

See also Court Records; Health and Welfare Records: State Orphanage (Owatonna)

Adoption records contain information about the adopted individual, birth parents, and adoptive parents. These records are part of the civil case files of the district courts.

Note: Adoption records are closed for 100 years from the date of adoption. Records that are less than 100 years old may be viewed only with a court order from the judge of the district court in which the adoption occurred.

American Indian Resources

The MHS collections are particularly rich in material about the two major Minnesota tribal groups: the Dakota (Sioux) and the Ojibwe (Chippewa). Collections include microfilms of U.S. Bureau of Indian Affairs records, as well as allotment papers, Indian rolls, censuses, land records, subject files, treaty papers, curricula, correspondence, reports, legal materials, newspaper clippings, railroad records, and other papers from American Indians, government officials, lawyers, missionaries, clergy, and others.

Significant publications include items about wars, folklore, religion, social customs, biography, and government relations and treaties, as well as such multi-volume works such as the *Annual Report of the Commissioner of Indian Affairs* (1839–1943) and the *Biographical and Historical Index of American Indians and Persons Involved in Indian Affairs* (U.S. Dept. of the Interior, 8 volumes).

Also consult the Visual Resources Database (at http://collections. mnhs.org/visualresources) for holdings of thousands of photographs of Minnesota Indian individuals, groups, and activities.

American Indian Census Rolls

See also Census Records

Microfilm of census rolls submitted each year by agents or superintendents in charge of reservations in Minnesota, or reservations in Wisconsin and North and South Dakota that had strong Minnesota con-

LEFT: *Sioux (Dakota) annuity roll entries recording payments from the federal government to members of Good Road's band of Mdewakanton Dakota Indians in present-day Bloomington, 1849*

nections. The data on the rolls varies but usually includes English and/or Indian name, roll number, age or birth date, sex, and relationship to head of family. There is not a census for every reservation or group of Indians for every year. Only persons who maintained a formal affiliation with a tribal group under federal supervision are listed in these census rolls.

Note: Microfilm (M559).

Chippewa and Sioux Annuity Rolls

Information about the Ojibwe (Chippewa), 1841–1907, and the Dakota (Sioux), 1849–1935, Indians who were paid annuities by the U.S. government under treaties negotiated between the tribal groups and the government. The rolls may give name of head of family; head's mark; number of men, women, children, and total number in each family; and amount of annuity paid.

Note: Microfilm (M390—Chippewa and M405—Sioux); available for interlibrary loan.

Dakota Conflict of 1862 Manuscripts Collections

A compilation of a variety of small collections of letters, reminiscences, reports, diaries, and other related materials dealing with Minnesota's Dakota Conflict of 1862 and related activities of 1862–65. The materials primarily detail the personal experiences of both white and Indian participants or witnesses, including raids and killings, construction of fortifications, hostages' experiences, the execution by the federal government at Mankato of 38 Dakota Indians found guilty of war crimes, and the subsequent and punitive expeditions led by Generals Henry H. Sibley and Alfred Sully into western Minnesota and Dakota Territory. A few items offer insight into the background and causes of the conflict (also known as the Dakota War and the Sioux Uprising).

Note: Microfilm (M582); available for interlibrary loan; available for sale from MHS to Minnesota residents and institutions and from Lexis-Nexis to non-Minnesota residents and institutions.

Native American Death Certificates

Unofficial death certificates, dated 1900, 1918–47 for Native Americans who either (1) died in Minnesota and were enrolled or otherwise connected with any Indian tribal groups or bands, or (2) died outside of Minnesota but were enrolled or otherwise connected with tribal groups or bands located in Minnesota. For those who died in Minnesota, these certificates may give additional or differing information from the official certificates. The records are arranged by state and within each state by Indian agency.

Note: Microfilm (SAM 401); available for interlibrary loan.

Biographical Resources
See also Family Histories

Biography Collection
Brief manuscripts containing miscellaneous information, arranged alphabetically by name, for more than 800 persons. Biographical and autobiographical sketches and notes, wedding and baptismal certificates, appointments, letters, reminiscences, school records, clippings, and memorial statements are included here when MHS does not hold an appropriate collection of personal or family papers.

Note: Ask staff for assistance.

Biography Files
See also Obituaries

Begun in 1917, this card file contains the names of about 100,000 persons, including farmers, doctors, educators, civic leaders, politicians, pioneer settlers, criminals, business executives, artists, actors, musicians, fashion designers, and authors. The references to persons are from newspapers, periodicals, and books within the MHS collections.

Approximately 9,000 of these entries are contained in the published volume "Minnesota Biographies, 1655–1912," compiled by Warren Upham and Rose Barteau Dunlap (*Collections of the Minnesota Historical Society,* volume 14; St. Paul: Minnesota Historical Society, 1912). The Minnesota Biographies Project began updating and enhancing the volume in 1976 and has added information for another 50,000 people. The MHS Library also has vertical files of miscellaneous newspaper clippings that contain biographical information; files are in order by surname.

Note: Ask staff for assistance.

Biography Reference Sets

The American Biographical-Genealogical Index (195 volumes, published since 1952) indexes every name in about 800 publications of family and local history and in the 1790 U.S. census. The MHS Library also has most of the titles included in this index.

Other significant publications include:

* *Dictionary of National Biography* (of Great Britain; 69 volumes covering 1885–1921)
* *Dictionary of American Biography* (20 original volumes, 1964 reprint has 11 volumes; 8 supplements)
* *Who's Who in America* (began publishing in 1899/1900)
* *Who Was Who in America* (covering 1607–1976; 7 volumes)
* *American Ancestry: Giving the Name and Descent, in the Male Line, of Americans Whose Ancestors Settled in the United States Previous to the Declaration of Independence, A.D. 1776* (12 volumes; published 1887–99)
* *Appleton's Cyclopædia of American Biography* (1887–89; 6 volumes, with volumes 7–11 published 1900–28 as supplementary editions)
* *Lamb's Biographical Dictionary of the United States* (7 volumes; published 1900–1903)
* *Genealogical Index* (of the Newberry Library, Chicago; 4 volumes; 1960)
* *Dictionary of Canadian Biography* (for persons possibly deceased by 1890; 11 volumes published, more in progress; index to volumes 1–4 published in 1981)
* *French-Canadian Families of the North Central States: A Genealogical Dictionary* (16 volumes; published 1980–)
* *Dictionnaire généalogique des familles Canadiennes depuis la fondation de la colonie jusqu'à nos jours* by Cyprien Tanguay (published 1871–90 in 7 volumes and reprinted in 1975; 3-volume supplement, *Complément au Dictionnaire généalogique Tanguay* by J.-Arthur Leboeuf, published 1957–64).

Birth Records

See also Municipal Records

Birth records in Minnesota vary in form, content, and location de-

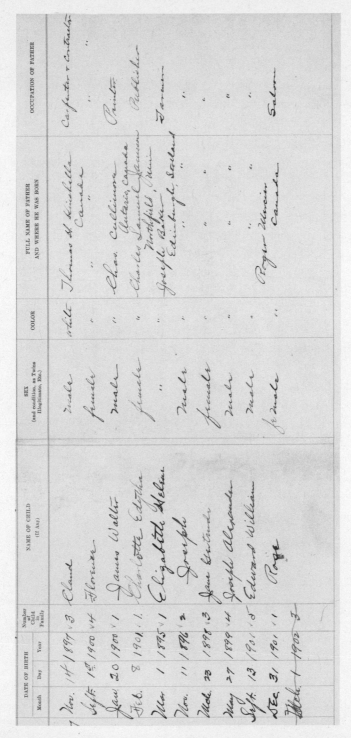

Part of entries in a register book of births in Koochiching (now International Falls), Itasca (now Koochiching) County, during 1897–1901

pending on the time period and jurisdiction in which the birth was reported. The records may be in the form of a one-line entry on a register
page or a certificate containing a great deal of data about the individual
and his/her birth. Although the extent of the content varies, it may include such information as the following: full name of child; date, time,
and place of birth; sex; color; name, age, and occupation of father;
maiden name and age of mother; parents' places of birth (usually state
or country only); name and address of attending physician or midwife;
and name of person reporting the birth. Birth records were recorded in
Minnesota townships, villages, and cities from 1870 to 1953 (longer in
cities of the first class: Minneapolis, St. Paul, and Duluth); in Minnesota's counties from 1870 to the present; and at the state Department
of Health from 1899 to the present.

Note: Microfilm (SAM 424—1899 birth registers); available for interlibrary loan. As of 2003, state-wide birth certificates for 1900–1934
are being imaged and indexed; check the MHS website for details.

Birth records are also retained in the county of record. MHS, in an
arrangement with the Genealogical Society of Utah, currently receives
microfilm of birth records from Minnesota counties. This project is far
from complete and as of 2003 only a few counties' birth records are
available on microfilm at MHS.

Note: Microfilm (check the on-line catalog for SAM numbers; each
county will have its own number); available for interlibrary loan. See
table on pages 95–99.

MHS also holds original birth registers from a number of Minnesota
townships and cities, dating from 1870 to 1953. Generally, these are
chronological listings, although some of the volumes include indexes
and reproduce the certificates. These sets are not complete, and many
jurisdictions are not represented. Township and city birth records may
not contain precisely the same information as the official birth
certificate.

Note: Search the on-line catalog under the county, township, or city
name and the subject birth records. Birth records may contain records
of out-of-wedlock or adoptive births that are restricted for 100 years;
consult the reference staff for availability.

Business Records
See also Public Service Department Records; Railroad Records

MHS holds unpublished collections of more than 600 businesses ranging in size from small grocery stores to multinational corporations. A few of these collections may contain payroll records and time books listing employee, employee number, job title, rate of pay, and hours worked. Annual reports, company newsletters, and employee newsletters also may contain information about individual employees.

Note: Access to some records may be restricted.

Company Newsletters
Newsletters produced by publicity and personnel departments and employee organizations. These may contain information about individual employees, as well as about retirements, mergers, awards, moves, investigations, and company policies. Some newsletters are cataloged as separate periodicals; others are included within the collections of particular businesses (Northwest Airlines or Great Northern Railway Company, for example).

Fur Trade Records
Daybooks, journals, ledgers, invoice books, business contracts, traders' accounts, diaries, correspondence, personal narratives, cargo manifests, and notary contracts. The records cover the North American fur trade from 1700 to the present and contain information about contracts between companies and individual traders, trading licenses, migration patterns, early settlements, and fur trade company and American Indian interactions. For information about early fur trade manuscript sources in the MHS collections and elsewhere, see *The Fur Trade in Minnesota: An Introductory Guide to Manuscript Sources* by Bruce M. White (St. Paul: Minnesota Historical Society, 1977). The guide includes a roster of early fur traders.

Incorporation Records
See also Church and Religious Organizations Resources

Articles of incorporation—filed with the Minnesota secretary of state—contain names, and occasionally addresses, of individuals who incorporated businesses. The State Archives holds several series including the main set of incorporation records (1858–1935) and specialized sets for state banks (1907–51), religious corporations (1885–1929), Catholic organizations (1877–1912), and cooperatives (1919–70), as well as a series of foreign (non-Minnesota) corporation records (1877–1913) that includes appointment of local agents in Minnesota.

Note: Indexes to active domestic corporations (SAM 117) and inactive domestic corporations (SAM 118) cover the period 1858 to 1986 and reflect active or inactive status as of 1986.

In addition, the secretary of state's website (at http://www.sos. state.mn.us/business/entities.html) includes a free, searchable database of Minnesota and non-Minnesota entities that have been dissolved or revoked.

Census Records

See also American Indian Resources: American Indian Census Rolls

Minnesota became a territory in 1849; the territorial period lasted until 1858. During this era, censuses were conducted in 1849, 1850 (federal), 1853, 1855, and 1857 (special federal census). While complete sets of the 1853 and 1855 censuses do not survive, listings for some counties are available.

Minnesota achieved statehood in 1858. After this date, the population of Minnesota was enumerated in two series of censuses: one by the federal government and another by the state of Minnesota. The federal censuses occurred in the years ending in "0," from 1860 through 1930. The Federal Data Privacy Act seals census records for 72 years. As of this writing, federal censuses taken after 1930 are not yet open for public use. The Minnesota state censuses were taken in 1865, 1875, 1885, 1895, and 1905.

Microfilm copies of both these series, as well as those taken during the territorial period, are available for research use at MHS. For each census year the censuses are arranged by county and then by community within the county. Individual names are not in alphabetical order. In rare instances, township or county copies of a census may also exist; ask staff for assistance with these copies.

Researchers should note that county and township boundaries and names changed frequently, especially in during the nineteenth century.

If the county or township appears to be missing, check under the name of the parent county or township.

Census types include:

- AGRICULTURAL CENSUS A typical Agricultural Census entry includes: name of owner, agent, or manager of farm; acres of land; cash value of farm; value of farming implements and machinery; number of livestock; produce harvested during year; value of animals slaughtered.
- MANUFACTURING CENSUS Commonly included in a Manufacturing Census entry are: name of corporation, company, or individual; name of business; capital invested; raw materials used; kind of motive power and machinery; average number of employees; wages; annual products and value.
- MORTALITY CENSUS A Mortality Census entry normally includes: name of the person who died in the preceding year; age; sex; color; free or slave; married or widowed; place of birth; month died; occupation; cause of death; and number of days ill.
- POPULATION CENSUS A typical Population Census entry includes: name; age; sex; color; occupation; value of real estate; birthplace (state or country); married within the year; attended school within the year; whether illiterate. Non-population censuses include the agricultural census, manufacturing census, mortality census, and social statistics census.
- SOCIAL STATISTICS CENSUS The Social Statistics Census lists by community the value of real and personal estate; annual taxes; crops; number and type of schools, libraries, newspapers, periodicals, and churches; pauperism; crime; and wages.

Note: Microfilm. MHS does not make interlibrary loans of National Archives microfilm of federal censuses, but does sell and loan microfilm of Minnesota state censuses. See individual entries below for details.

Minnesota Censuses
1820
POPULATION CENSUS
The earliest census listings for the area that later became Minnesota

are found in the 1820 Michigan territorial census. A print version of the Michigan territorial census of 1820 is also available.

1830
POPULATION CENSUS

None of the 1830 territorial censuses seem to include Minnesota.

1836
POPULATION CENSUS

The 1836 Wisconsin territorial census includes portions of present-day Minnesota as part of Crawford County and as part of Dubuque County (later in Iowa Territory). A print version of the Wisconsin territorial censuses is also available for research.

1838
POPULATION CENSUS

Portions of Minnesota are also in the 1838 Wisconsin Territory census as part of Crawford and Clayton counties. A print version of the Wisconsin territorial censuses is also available for research.

1840
POPULATION CENSUS

Minnesota inhabitants are included in the 1840 Wisconsin and Iowa territorial censuses. A print version of the Wisconsin territorial censuses is also available for research.

1849, 1850, 1853, 1855 Censuses

The censuses of 1849, 1853, and 1855 were special censuses conducted by the government of Minnesota Territory; the census of 1850 was a standard federal decennial census conducted by the U.S. Census Office. MHS has microfilmed manuscript and published versions of the population and non-population census schedules and related materials for Minnesota Territory for those years. All four years are available on one roll of microfilm, which is available for sale and interlibrary loan. In addition, MHS has a copy of the National Archives microfilm of the 1850 population census, which is not available for sale or interlibrary loan.

1849

POPULATION CENSUS

Name of head of household; number of males; number of females. Despite governmental instructions to the contrary, some Indian people were listed in the population censuses of 1849 and 1850. Published in Minnesota (Territory), Legislative Assembly, *Journal of the House of Representatives*, First Session of the Territory of Minnesota, 1850. Also on microfilm (on roll with 1850, 1853, and 1855 censuses); available for sale and interlibrary loan.

1850

AGRICULTURAL CENSUS

Covers twelve months preceding June 1, 1850. On microfilm (on roll with 1849, 1853, and 1855 censuses); available for sale and interlibrary loan.

MANUFACTURING CENSUS

Covers twelve months preceding June 1, 1850. On microfilm (on roll with 1849, 1853, and 1855 censuses); available for sale and interlibrary loan.

MORTALITY CENSUS

Covers twelve months preceding June 1, 1850. On microfilm (on roll with 1849, 1853, and 1855 censuses); available for sale and interlibrary loan.

POPULATION CENSUS

Official census date: June 1, 1850. The MHS microfilm edition of the 1850 population census consists of the county copies and the territory/state copy of the census. MHS also has a copy of the National Archives microfilm roll containing the federal copy of this census. Despite governmental instructions to the contrary, some Indian people were listed in the population censuses of 1849 and 1850. For a published census and surname index, see *Minnesota Territorial Census, 1850*, edited by Patricia C. Harpole and Mary D. Nagle (St. Paul: Minnesota Historical Society, 1972). On MHS microfilm (on roll with 1849, 1853, and 1855 censuses); available for sale and interlibrary loan.

SOCIAL STATISTICS CENSUS

Covers twelve months preceding June 1, 1850. On microfilm (on roll with 1849, 1853, and 1855 censuses); available for sale and interlibrary loan.

1853

POPULATION CENSUS *(Incomplete)*

Name of the head of household; number of children; number in household; names of inhabitants (for some communities only). On microfilm (on roll with 1849, 1850, and 1855 censuses); available for sale and interlibrary loan.

1855

POPULATION CENSUS *(Incomplete)*

Name of the head of household; number of males; number of females; total number in household. On microfilm (on roll with 1849, 1850, and 1853 censuses); available for sale and interlibrary loan.

1857

POPULATION CENSUS

Includes voting status of males (native or naturalized), and the occupation of each male over the age of 15. Official census date: September 21, 1857. There is a microfilm index by surname, which is available for sale and interlibrary loan.

1860

AGRICULTURAL CENSUS

Covers twelve months preceding June 1, 1860. Available for sale and interlibrary loan.

MANUFACTURING CENSUS

Covers twelve months preceding June 1, 1860. Available for sale and interlibrary loan.

MORTALITY CENSUS

Covers twelve months preceding June 1, 1860. Available for sale and interlibrary loan.

POPULATION CENSUS

Also includes value of personal estate; deaf, dumb, blind, insane, pauper, and convicts. Official census date: June 1, 1860. There is a published index by surname. During the 1930s, the Work Projects Administration (WPA) compiled a card index to the 1860 census, which MHS microfilmed. The card index is available for sale and interlibrary loan. For more information on the 1860 census, see *Guide to the Use of the 1860 Minnesota Population Census Schedules and Index* by Dennis E. Meissner

(St. Paul: Division of Archives and Manuscripts, Minnesota Historical Society, 1978).

SOCIAL STATISTICS CENSUS

Covers twelve months preceding June 1, 1860. Available for sale and interlibrary loan.

1865

POPULATION CENSUS

Also includes whether deaf, dumb, blind, or insane; and soldiers in service on June 1, 1865. Official census date: June 1, 1865. Available for sale and interlibrary loan.

1870

AGRICULTURAL CENSUS

Also includes amount of wages paid, and estimated value of all farm production. Covers twelve months preceding June 1, 1870. Available for sale and interlibrary loan.

MANUFACTURING CENSUS

Also includes number of months in active operation, and materials and value. Covers twelve months preceding June 1, 1870. Available for sale and interlibrary loan.

MORTALITY CENSUS

Also includes if father and mother were foreign born; omits free or slave and number of days ill. Covers twelve months preceding June 1, 1870. Available for sale and interlibrary loan.

POPULATION CENSUS

Also notes if father and mother were foreign born; month of birth or marriage if occurred within the last year; male citizens of United States age 21 and over; and male citizens whose right to vote was denied. Official census date: June 1, 1870. A microfilmed card index—compiled by MHS staff members—is arranged by county and by surname within county. Microfilm of the card index is available for sale and interlibrary loan. A partial published index by surname gives page numbers for family entry and for agricultural entry; see *Minnesota 1870 Census Index*, edited by Ronald Vern Jackson (Salt Lake City: Accelerated Indexing Systems, 1979).

SOCIAL STATISTICS CENSUS

Also includes amount of public debt. Covers twelve months preceding June 1, 1870. Available for sale and interlibrary loan.

1875

POPULATION CENSUS

Official census date: May 1, 1875. There is no index. Available for sale and interlibrary loan.

1880

AGRICULTURAL CENSUS

Also notes cost of fences; cost of fertilizer; weeks of hired labor; poultry; and forest products. Covers twelve months preceding June 1, 1880. Available for sale and interlibrary loan.

MANUFACTURING CENSUS

Plus greatest number of persons employed at one time. Available for sale and interlibrary loan.

MORTALITY CENSUS

Also includes marital status; birthplaces of father and mother (state or country); length of residence in county; place where taken ill if other county; and name of attending physician. Covers twelve months preceding June 1, 1880. Available for sale and interlibrary loan.

POPULATION CENSUS

Includes for the first time name of street; house number; relation of each person to head of household; marital status; number of months unemployed in previous year; whether ill or injured on day of enumeration; birthplaces of father and mother (state or country). Official census date: June 1, 1880. A microfilm Soundex index (arranged phonetically by surname) lists only households with children under age of 10. For a partial published index, see *Minnesota 1880 Census Index*, edited by Ronald Vern Jackson (North Salt Lake City, Utah: Accelerated Indexing Systems, 1985).

RIGHT: *The 1875 Minnesota state census for Redwood County includes Charles and Caroline Ingalls and their daughters Mary, Carrie, and Laura, who as Laura Ingalls Wilder later wrote the famous Little House books for children. On the Banks of Plum Creek is based on the family's experiences of living in a riverbank dugout near Walnut Grove in North Hero Township during the 1870s.*

Families numbered	Name of every person whose residence was in this family on the 1st of May, 1875.	Age	Sex	Color	Nativity, State or Country.	Parent Nativity. Father.	Parent Nativity. Mother.
1	Lewis Juhnson	47	M	W	Germany	Ger.	Ger.
	Anna Y. Juhnson	57	F	W	"	"	"
2	C. D. Ingalls	39	M	W	N.Y.	Ger.	N.Y.
	Caroline Ingalls	35	F	W	Wis.	Mass.	Mass.
	Mary C. D. Ingalls	10	F	W	Wis	N.Y.	Wis
	Laura C. Ingalls	8	F	W	"	"	"
	Carrie C. Ingalls	5	F	W	Kan.	"	"
3	C. G. Thompson	32	M	W	Ger.	Scotland	Scotland
	Sarah Thompson	31	F	W	N.Y	Eng.	Eng.
	Lottie Thompson	5	F	W	Wis	Ger.	Ger.
	William Thompson	3	M	W	"	"	"
	G. W. Thompson	1	M	W	N.Y	"	"
4	John Edwin	52	M	W	N.Y	"	Ireland

SOCIAL STATISTICS CENSUS

Provides information about homeless children; prisoners; paupers and indigents; deaf-mutes; blind; insane; and idiots. Covers twelve months preceding June 1, 1880. Available for sale and interlibrary loan.

1885

POPULATION CENSUS

Instead of parents' birthplaces, census notes if father and mother are of foreign birth; plus deaf, dumb, blind, insane; and soldiers in the Civil War. Official census date: May 1, 1885. There is no index. Available for sale and interlibrary loan.

1890

POPULATION CENSUS

Most of the United States population census was destroyed by fire in 1921. For Minnesota, one page for Rockford Township, Wright County, survived (available on roll 3 of the 1890 census microfilm). The local copy for Rockville Township, Stearns County, also survived.

VETERANS CENSUS

Includes the name of the surviving veteran or widow; rank; company; regiment or vessel; date of enlistment; date of discharge; length of service; post office address; disability incurred; and remarks. For a partial published index by surname, see *1890 Minnesota Census Index of Civil War Veterans or Their Widows*, compiled by Bryan Lee Dilts (Salt Lake City: Index Pub., 1985).

1895

POPULATION CENSUS

For first time includes length of residence in state and enumeration district (years and months) of males; occupation; months regularly employed in previous year; if previously enumerated in census; omits deaf, dumb, blind, insane. Official census date: June 1, 1895. Index in progress; ask staff for assistance. Census available for sale and interlibrary loan.

1900

POPULATION CENSUS

Includes month and year of birth; mother of how many children and number of children living; year of immigration to the United States;

number of years in the U.S.; whether naturalized; literacy; English speaking; and ownership of home. Official census date: June 1, 1900. Microfilm index (Soundex)—arranged phonetically by surname—lists all households.

1905

POPULATION CENSUS

Includes street address; birthplaces of father and mother (state or country); length of residence for each person; service in Civil and Spanish-American Wars. Official census date: June 1, 1905. There is no index, but ask staff for help when searching Duluth, Minneapolis, or St. Paul. Available for sale and interlibrary loan.

1910

POPULATION CENSUS

Also notes length of marriage; language spoken; type of industry employed in; if employer, employee, or self-employed; number of weeks unemployed in 1909; if unemployed on April 15, 1910; if a survivor of the Union or Confederate armies or navies. Official census date: April 15, 1910. There is no index, but ask staff for help when searching Duluth, Minneapolis, or St. Paul.

1920

POPULATION CENSUS

Also includes year of immigration to the U.S.; whether naturalized and year of naturalization; school attendance; literacy; birthplace of person and parents; mother tongue of foreign born; ability to speak English; occupation, industry, and class of worker; home owned or rented; if owned, whether mortgaged; for non-farm, mortgaged, market value, original amount of mortgage, balance due, and interest rate. Official census date: January 1, 1920. Microfilm index (Soundex)—arranged phonetically by surname—includes all households.

1930

POPULATION CENSUS

Also includes age at first marriage; year of immigration to the United States; naturalization status; birthplace (state or country only); mother tongue of father and mother; ability to speak English; occupation;

whether a veteran and of which war. Official census date: April 1, 1930. There is no index, but ask staff for help.

Non-Minnesota Censuses

In addition to the Minnesota federal and state censuses, MHS holds for other states a miscellaneous collection of published censuses and in- dexes, as well as microfilms. Full runs of censuses include, for example, complete 1790 United States census; 1830 Michigan Territory census; 1836, 1850, and 1860 Wisconsin territorial and state censuses; 1840 and 1860 Iowa territorial and state censuses; 1860, 1870, and 1880 Dakota Territory census; 1885 Dakota Territory census for the area that became North Dakota in 1889.

Church and Religious Organizations Resources

See also Business Records: Incorporation Records; Marriage Records; Newspapers; Oral Histories; Work Projects Administration (WPA) Re- sources

General Collections

MHS has resources primarily for Christian and Jewish denominations, as well as for a few other religious groups. Records of Christian churches in Minnesota may include baptisms, marriages, funerals, and other sacraments; lists of members; minutes of congregational or parish meet- ings and of women's, laymen's, and youth organizations; constitutions and bylaws; financial records; Sunday School records; bulletins; an- niversary publications; and reports by, and biographical information about, ministers or priests. Synagogue / temple records contain simi- lar types of information relevant to Jewish religious traditions. While MHS holds records for many individual congregations in Minnesota, it has only a very small number of those that have existed in the state. Most records remain within their institutions.

    Note: Some records are on microfilm; available for sale and inter- library loan.

Printed Histories

General histories of Christian denominations, histories of specific con- gregations and/or churches and Jewish synagogues and temples, minutes of annual meetings, and church bulletins and periodicals. A general history of Methodism in Minnesota, for example, will focus on the more prominent men and women of that denomination. Jubilee or anniversary booklets often include such items as membership lists and the names of confirmation-class members and the clergy. Minutes of a denomination's annual meeting may include names of newly ordained ministers, persons licensed to preach, names and residences of current clergy, lists of delegates to the meeting, and biographies of recently deceased clergy. Church bulletins and periodicals may contain information about weekly or monthly activities. MHS's published holdings on Jewish history include anniversary histories of synagogues and temples, dedications of new buildings, and directories.

Note: Search the on-line catalog by name of denomination or name of individual church, synagogue, or temple.

Episcopal Church Records

Documentation of the organization, administration, function, and history of the Episcopal Church, Diocese of Minnesota, and its parishes, missions (including Minnesota American Indian mission churches), officials, and leaders. The records include parish histories, historical information, financial and organizational records, sermons, lectures, minutes, diaries, clippings, biographical information, scrapbooks, and reports, as well as some parish records.

Roman Catholic Records

Questionnaires sent in 1948 by the Catholic Archdiocese of St. Paul and Minneapolis—covering Minnesota, North Dakota, and South Dakota—to each of its parishes. The questionnaires gathered information about persons, events, and dates significant in parish history; inventories of parish records; buildings; cemeteries; parish organizations; parochial school programs; and the ethnic composition and geographical origins of parish members. Many parishes sent additional information such as anniversary celebration materials. These materials may be in languages other than English. The questionnaires do not include actual sacramental records (baptisms, marriages, funerals).

Note: Microfilm (M260); available for sale and interlibrary loan. The records are organized alphabetically—by name of state, within each state by name of city, and within each city by name of parish.

United Church of Christ Records

Records documenting the organization, functions, congregations, and administration of the Minnesota Conference of the United Church of Christ and its predecessor organizations, the Congregational Conference of Minnesota and the Evangelical and Reformed Church, Northern Synod. Included are records of several organizations, such as women's, laymen's, and youth groups; records of geographical subdivisions of the state organization; and the administration records of the Conference. Records of some individual churches are included.

WPA Historical Records Survey of Churches

Information gathered by the Work Projects Administration (WPA) in the late 1930s and early 1940s. The church history form includes name, denomination, and location of church; date established; any denominational or name changes; names of present officers; number of original members; number of present members; information about church buildings; names of pastors and dates of service; church cemetery; languages used for services; publications; and official records of church and its organizations. The records are not complete for the entire state.

Commission of Public Safety Records

The Minnesota Commission of Public Safety, established by the legislature in April 1917, was given broad powers to ensure protection of persons and property, defense of the state and the nation, and application of the state's resources to "successful prosecution" of World War I. The commission was very active until most of its orders were rescinded in February 1919. It tied up its affairs in 1921. The commission ordered the establishment of the Home Guard of Minnesota, the Minnesota Motor Corps Division, and a corps of emergency local peace officers.

The commission issued 59 executive orders, which dealt with the regulation of liquor traffic, dance halls, and poolrooms; and provided for the registration of aliens and their property holdings, a farm crop and labor census, regulation of milk prices and the manufacture and distribution of bread, a statewide barberry eradication program, creation of municipal wood yards, and prohibitions against the employment of aliens as teachers and the use of foreign languages in schools.

The commission also formed an employment bureau, a speakers bureau, and a publicity bureau, which provided material to local newspapers, distributed pamphlets and leaflets in several languages, and published a weekly bulletin, *Minnesota in the War*. It also supported the Liberty Chorus and community sing movement.

Alien Registration Records

A February 1918 listing of all non-U.S. citizens in Minnesota, excluding most Germans, conducted by order of the Minnesota Commission of Public Safety. The two-page form includes information about a person's place and date of birth, port of entry and date of arrival in the United States, occupation, names and ages of children, financial situation, and male relatives taking part in World War I. The collection has been indexed, and both the index and the forms are on microfilm.

Note: Microfilm (SAM 169; indexed by SAM 169-I); available for sale and interlibrary loan.

Americanization Survey Cards (Ramsey County)

A 1918 survey of families in St. Paul with names of family members; ward, precinct, and block number; church; lodge; and newspaper subscriptions. The information about each person more than 16 years of age includes age, sex, country of birth, race or nationality, years in the United States, citizenship status, whether English is spoken or written, whether any other language is spoken or written, marital status, birthplaces of father and mother, where attending English classes, physical defects, and occupation. For each person younger than 16 the survey also includes information about last school and grade attended.

Note: Microfilm (SAM 220); available for sale and interlibrary loan. The cards are not indexed.

Farm Crop and Labor Reports

Reports include name of farmer, address, nearest shipping point, name of railroad, nationality or descent of farmer, kind of crops and acres

Alien Registration and Declaration of Holdings

Serial Number

This registration blank to be forwarded to J. A. O. Preus, State Auditor, Saint Paul, Minnesota.

Rock   County *Ash Creek*   Town / Village / City

1. Full name of Alien Registrant _Henry Kloosterboer_
2. Street Address, Postoffice Box or R. F. D. Route
3. Village, City or Town _Ash Creek_
4. Length of residence at the foregoing place _7 years_
5. Give Age Last Birthday _71_
6. To what country do you claim allegiance? _Germany_
7. Where Born _Germany_
8. Date of Birth _January 23, 1847_
9. Port of entry to United States _New York_
10. Date of Arrival in United States _May 3, 1903_
11. Married? _Yes_   12. Is Wife living? _Yes_
13. Residence of wife, if living _With husband_
14. Do you speak and write English? _No_
15. Have you a trade or profession, and what? _No._
16. In exactly what line of work are you at present engaged? _None_
17. Give names and ages of all living children, and state which are attending public schools.
Harry Kloosterboer 44, Rudolph Kloosterboer 42, Gertrude (Kloosterboer) Ubben, 40, Henry Kloosterboer 32, Anton Kloosterboer 30.
18. Have any of your male relatives taken part in present war either for or against the United States and its allies? If answer yes, give name, relationship, and state which country served? _Yes Youst Wessels & Harry Kloosterboer. Nephews serving Germany._
19. Did you register under selective draft, and if so, where? _No_
20. What is your serial number?
21. Did you claim exemption from military service and why?
22. Have you ever taken out first papers of naturalization in the United States? If so, state where and date _No_
23. If you have taken out first papers of naturalization why have you not taken out second papers?

Alien Registration and Declaration of Holdings form of 1918 for Henry Kloosterboer of Ash Creek, a 71-year-old native of Germany who had arrived in the United States in 1903

planted in 1917 and 1918, livestock and number of each kind, number of silos, and report of farm labor needs. Individual reports are not extant for all counties.

Note: Microfilm (SAM 217); available for sale and interlibrary loan. The records are not indexed, but are arranged by county, then alphabetically by surname of farmer.

Women in Industry Survey

Information—compiled by the Minnesota Commission of Public Safety's Women's Committee, in cooperation with the Minnesota Department of Labor and Industry's Bureau of Women and Children—about firms employing women and about individual female employees in 1918. The information about a firm includes wages, hours, and working conditions. The information about an employee includes name, age, country of birth, nationality, kind of work, wages per week, whether living at home, whether contributing to family support, marital status, whether son or husband is in war service, husband's present employment, husband's wages per week, and ages of children. A separate history sheet for married women with dependents gives employee's name; age; country of birth; marital status; family information, including child care; name of employer; distance of workplace from home; income; and relief needs. There are no forms for the following counties: Clearwater, Jackson, Mahnomen, Meeker, Sibley, and Traverse. Also, there are no forms for the city of Duluth.

Note: Microfilm (SAM 222); available for sale and interlibrary loan. The records are arranged by names of county and employer. They are not indexed.

Cookbooks

Cookbooks can be an unexpected source of information for genealogists. Used in conjunction with published congregational histories, they can provide information on family members who were members of a church Ladies Aid or synagogue women's group. They can show which recipes family members submitted to the charitable cookbooks published by many churches and synagogues to raise funds. They can also indicate other organizational affiliations and memberships, from the

Fridley Skating Club to the Minneapolis Institute of Arts. Ethnic cookbooks in the MHS collections provide recipes from a number of groups, from the ubiquitous Scandinavians to the more recent Koreans and Hmong.

Families have begun to publish cookbooks, often in connection with family reunions. These are of two main types: those that honor a particular cook in the family, often a grandmother, and those that solicit recipes from all family members. Many include photographs, family stories, even family trees. Families that have operated food-related businesses such as butcher shops and restaurants might also find that the businesses have published cookbooks.

Court Records
See also Adoption Records; Divorce Records

Civil Case Files
Documents relating to matters brought before the court, including monetary matters, changes of name, divorces, garnishments, and adoptions. The files may include complaint, answer, summons, findings, and judgment. Files generally do not include trial transcripts. Most case file indexes are still held by the district court administrator.

Note: Some files are restricted; ask staff for assistance.

Criminal Case Files
Documents relating to criminal proceedings, including murder, larceny, battery, and embezzlement charges. Individual files may contain warrants, subpoenas, verdicts, and sentencing information if the person was convicted. The State of Minnesota is listed as the plaintiff. Cases for some counties are interfiled with civil cases. Files generally do not include trial transcripts. Most case file indexes are still held by the district court administrator.

Death Records
See also Municipal Records; Obituaries

Death Certificates and Cards

Death records in Minnesota vary in form, content, and location depending on the time period and the jurisdiction in which the death was reported. The records may be in the form of a one-line entry on a register page, an individual card containing data on each death, or a

Minnesota Department of Health death certificate for Wiley Roger Pope, a genealogist and long-time librarian at the Minnesota Historical Society who died in 1990

certificate containing a great deal of data about the individual and his/her death. Although the extent of the content varies depending on the time period and informant, it may include such information as the following: full name of deceased, full date and time of death, jurisdiction of death, sex, color/race, age, marital status, usual residence, occupation, date and place of birth, parents' names and places of birth, spouse's name, military service (if any), Social Security number, name and address of informant, primary and secondary causes of death, name and address of physician and dates of attendance by the physician, place and date of burial, cremation or removal of body, and name and address of the undertaker handling the arrangements.

Death records were recorded in Minnesota townships, villages, and cities from 1870 to 1953 (longer in the cities of the first class: Minneapolis, St. Paul, and Duluth); in Minnesota's counties from 1870 to the present; and at the state Department of Health from 1899 to the present. Beginning in 1908, the state Department of Health's copy was declared the "official" record of death.

Note: Microfilm: MHS has the following microfilm copies of records maintained by the state Department of Health: death registers, 1899; death cards, 1900–1907; and death certificates, 1908–96. The certificates and cards from 1906 through 1996 are indexed through a searchable on-line database available at http://people.mnhs.org/dci/Search.cfm. The microfilm may be searched in person at MHS or borrowed through interlibrary loan. These services are explained in the Frequently Asked Questions (FAQs) that accompany the search site.

Cemetery Records

See also Health and Welfare Records: Public Hospitals/Facilities Records; Military and Veterans' Records: Veterans' Grave Registrations; Municipal Records; Prison Records; Work Projects Administration (WPA) Resources

Of interest to genealogists are burial records, cemetery plats, indexes to burials in hospital cemeteries and municipally owned cemeteries, obituary records, and listings of burials from Minnesota's state hospitals. Notable hospitals include Faribault State School and Hospital, Willmar State Hospital, Hastings State Hospital, Cambridge State Hospital, and St. Peter State Hospital.

Minnesota Department of Health records include an incomplete 1933 statewide cemetery inventory listing the location and name of the cemetery and the name and address of the secretary or person in charge. In the late 1930s the Historical Records Survey of the Work Projects Administration (WPA) conducted a survey that has information about many Minnesota cemeteries, including private and Indian burials and abandoned cemeteries. The survey form includes name of cemetery; county; township, village or city; location; ownership; date established; date of first burial; dedication date; condition and history of cemetery; location of records; and source of information. The forms, which are arranged by county, do not list persons buried in the cemeteries.

Inscriptions have been copied from gravestones in cemeteries located in most of Minnesota's counties. Complete lists for some counties have been published. Some inscriptions from practically all counties have been copied and published. Many inscriptions have been published in periodical articles and are not listed separately in the online catalog.

Coroner Records/Reports

Records of some county coroner offices giving name of deceased person, conclusion as to cause of death, name of coroner, and other relevant information; may also contain records of an inquest. The certificates are filed by the county coroner in the district court.

Note: Some records are indexed. Access to some information may be restricted.

Corpse Permits

Record of permits (1898–1912) issued for the transportation of corpses, primarily to other states, although there were some intrastate shipments. Each register entry lists number and date of permit, name of deceased, date and cause of death, destination, name of medical attendant, name of health officer, name of undertaker, name of escort, and railroad company transporting the corpse.

Note: The permits are not indexed.

County/Township Death Records

Most death records prior to 1908 are retained in the county of record. MHS, in an arrangement with the Genealogical Society of Utah, is currently filming county/township death records from Minnesota counties. The project is far from completion, and only a few counties have been filmed. As of 2003, MHS holds county death records on microfilm for only: Anoka, Brown, Dodge, Faribault, Isanti, Kandiyohi, Martin, Mower, Olmsted, Steele, Wadena, Waseca, and Washington Counties.

MHS also holds original death registers from a number of Minnesota townships and cities, dating from 1870 to 1953. Generally, these are chronological listings, although some of the volumes include indexes. These sets are not complete, and many jurisdictions are not represented. Township and city death records may not contain precisely the same information as the official death certificate.

Note: GSU microfilm of county death records is available for interlibrary loan. See table on pages 95–99.

Native American Death Certificates

Unofficial death certificates, dated 1900, 1918–47 for Native Americans who either (1) died in Minnesota and were enrolled or otherwise connected with any Indian tribal groups or bands, or (2) died outside of Minnesota but were enrolled or otherwise connected with tribal groups or bands located in Minnesota. For those who died in Minnesota, these certificates may give additional or differing information from the official certificates. The records are arranged by state and within each state by Indian agency.

Note: Microfilm (SAM 401); available for interlibrary loan.

Obituaries

Generally, small-town newspapers publish more detailed obituaries that may include the places and dates of birth and marriage, survivors, and biographical information. In larger cities, particularly Minneapolis and St. Paul, the older daily newspapers did not publish obituaries as they do today. If a death notice was printed, it was more often a notice of only the funeral. Researchers should be aware that obituaries were not found in only one section of the newspaper as they are today.

Probate Records

Will books, final decrees of distribution of estates, and some order books, as well as indexes to wills and decrees. Records of insanity hearings and

GOES TO SLEEP; WAKES IN ANOTHER WORLD

K. C. JOHNSON, PROMINENT HART-LAND FARMER, PASSES AWAY.

Is Victim of Heart Failure—Apparently in Good Health, and Goes Without Warning — He Leaves a Large Family.

Another prominent citizen of Hartland township has been called upon to answer the sudden and unexpected summons of the grim reaper. Knute C. Johnson, apparently in usual good health, went to sleep Monday night to awaken in another and better world. He passed away without warning, without a chance to say farewell to the members of his family. About five o'clock Tuesday morning his wife was awakened when he attempted to raise up in bed; she heard him gasp twice and then he sank back lifeless upon the pillow. She aroused the family and Dr. Garlock was summoned by phone and arrived in a very short time, but Mr. Johnson was beyond help. The doctor pronounced death due to heart failure.

Mr. Johnson had been troubled with an annoying cough but otherwise had been in normal health, attended to the farm work as usual and on the Saturday previous had returned from Minneapolis where he had been in attendance at the Sonod church meeting.

In this death the township and county lose one of their most prominent farmers and highly respected citizens, a man whose life, since the age of one year, has been spent on the beautiful home farm on Mule lake, a life which was unobtrusive, contented with things as they were, uncomplaining. His friends speak of him as a good neighbor, friendly and obliging, always ready to lend a helping hand to others, a dependable man in every sense of the word, true always to whatever he thought was right. He was the head of a large family among the members of which his gentleness and fatherly interest won for him the greatest love and respect. His unexpected and untimely death is a sad blow to the wife and children who have the sympathy of many friends in their bereavement.

Knute C. Johnson was born in Madison, Dane county, Wis., on April 29, 1860; died in Hartland township June 17, 1913, age 53 yrs, 1 month and 18 days. When he was one year old his parents, Mr. and Mrs. Carl Johnson, moved to this county and located upon the farm on Mule lake. On March 8, 1885, he was married to Miss Gunild Burtness, of New Richland, and to this union twelve children were born, all of whom, with the mother, survive. The children are Mrs. Othelia Mellang, of Albert Lea, Lena, Clara, Oscar, Gilmore, Cargia, Lydia, Albert, Reuben, Warner, Georgia, and Cordelia, at home.

Deceased is survived by three brothers and two sisters, J. C. Johnson and C. C. Johnson, of Hartland, Edwin Johnson of Golden Valley, Minn., Mrs. B. C. Siblerud and Mrs. Peter Hanson, of Hartland. One sister, Mrs. A. Siblerud, of New Richland, preceded him in death.

Mr. Johnson was a lifelong member of the Synod Lutheran church and was trustee of the Hartland church at the time of his death.

Funeral services will be held at the house at 10 o'clock Saturday morning and at the Synod church in Hartland afterward.

An especially informative newspaper obituary for farmer Knute C. Johnson of Hartland Township, Freeborn County, from the Hartland Herald, June 20, 1913

Last Will and Testament of Philip Martineau. deceased.

I. the undersigned Philip Martineau. of the town of Ripley Morrison County Minnesota. Being mindful of the uncertainty of this life. and of the certainty of death. being of sound mind and memory. do hereby make and declare this writing to be my last will and testament.

First. I request that all of the expenses of my funeral and just debts shall be paid.

Second. I will and bequeath to Joseph Martineau all the land I own in Section seven. (7) Town forty-two. (42) North of Range thirty-one (31) West in Morrison County. State of Minnesota.

Third. I give and bequeath to Clara Duro. one cow. and fifty dollars. in money.

Fourth I give and bequeath to said Joseph Martineau all of the property that I may have at my death not herein mentioned.

Dated at Little Falls. Minnesota this 28th day of April 1901.

Philip X Martineau
his
mark

We Edman Duro. and Charles Stewart now in the presence of Philip Martineau who signes the above and foregoing Will. at his request do hereby sign our names as witnesses to said Will all of which is written on this sheet.

Names of witnesses Edman X Duro. post Ripley Minn Charles Stewart. Little Falls Minn.
his
mark

Will book entry for Philip Martineau of Ripley Township, Morrison County, 1901

commitments from some probate courts are in the State Archives, as are letters of administration (usually pre-1880 only), minutes, records regarding guardianships and conservatorships, and wills from many county probate courts.

Matters heard by the probate court in each county vary by jurisdiction and over time. Probate courts traditionally have had jurisdiction over settlements of estates and over guardianships of minors and incompetents (this has included insanity hearings and commitments). They formerly heard many family matters now handled by the family division of the district court.

Note: While probate case files generally are retained by the courts, some records have been microfilmed and are available for sale and interlibrary loan. Not all probate records, however, are on microfilm. See table on pages 95–99. Law restricts access to insanity and juvenile records.

Directories

See also Public Service Department Records

Business Directories

MHS has major holdings of gazetteers and business directories, for the late-nineteenth and early-twentieth centuries, that cover Minnesota and often North Dakota, South Dakota, and Montana as well. Alphabetical arrangement is by community name; in addition to names of individuals and their business category or firm name, information may include when the community was established and its location and population. Each volume contains a reverse listing by business category. Many individual business directories for the state or a city are also available, the earliest publication being dated 1865. These directories do not list employees of a business.

City Directories

Name listings of persons residing in a city, with occupation and address; generally provided for large cities only. Some directories list removals to other cities as well as death dates. By 1930 city directories include a wife's name in the entry for her husband and a reverse listing under street address. *The Dual City Blue Book* (18 volumes; St. Paul: R. L. Polk & Co., 1885–1923) covers St. Paul and Minneapolis basically as a social register and includes a reverse directory by address.

Directories for many Minneapolis and St. Paul suburban areas are available from the 1970s to present. Some directories include small communities within a larger city's vicinity, or all communities in the county, as well as farmers of the county. There are not complete sets of directories for every city.

Professional Directories

State or national guides to members of professions, such as law or teaching. Often these directories list individuals' names, addresses, year of admittance or license for profession, college attended, and year of degree.

Rural Directories

See also Maps and Other Geographical Resources

Directories of farmers found as part of a county plat book (see also the section on plat books under Maps and Other Geographical Information) or as part of county or city/county directory. The information may include name, section, township, number of acres, value of property, and post office. In addition, some early gazetteers list farmers in selected Minnesota counties.

Telephone Directories

The majority of telephone directories for Minnesota cities begin in the 1940–50 period with the exception of ones for St. Paul and Minneapolis, which began as a combined directory in 1915. Telephone directories for earlier years do not give as complete a listing of residents as do city directories, because telephones were not found in every home. MHS does not have telephone directories for non-Minnesota cities.

Note: Ask staff for assistance.

Disaster Relief Records

See also Farm Records: Drought Relief Applications, Hail Relief Applications

The MHS collections contain information about major disasters that have occurred in Minnesota and their aftermaths. This information cov-

Ledger Page 189.

Registration Blank.

Name _Irish Jennie_ Miss W Birth place _Wis_

Wifes Name _____, Birth place _____

Children, _____, Birth place _____

Residence _Hinckley_, How long _4 mo_, How long in Minnesota _2 years in Duluth_

Occupation _Cook_.

Did he own his home _____. If mortgaged, for how much.

$ _____. How much insurance $ _____.

What property left _only clothing on her back_,

Value $ _____.

Address of friends _None_

Ability of _____

Needs _Clothing & Trans to W Supr_

Wants to go to _West Superior_
Staying at Mrs Wilcox's

Aid registration form for Jennie Irish, a survivor of the Hinckley forest fire of 1894 that destroyed the city, killed at least 413 people, and burned approximately 160,000 acres of timberland

ers such items as the snowstorms of 1871–73; seed grain program distribution requests (grasshopper relief), 1874 and 1877; Argyle hailstorm, 1886–87; the Hinckley, Milaca, New York Mills, and Sandstone fires, 1894; and the Chisholm, Moose Lake-Cloquet fire relief, 1918. The information may include name of person requesting relief; locality; legal description of property; marital status and number of children; nature of loss; plight of surviving family members; crops and livestock destroyed; photographs, plans, and specifications for replacement buildings; relief registrations; donations, amount of relief allowed, date of payment, in what manner paid, and remarks.

Note: The records are not indexed.

Divorce Records

See also Court Records

Divorce records are found among the district court records in the county where the divorce was finalized. The case file will be contained in the civil case file series, usually arranged in numerical order. The case file usually contains copies of all documents entered into the court record, including the original petition, any orders for support and maintenance, motions and documents filed by the plaintiff and defendant, investigation reports ordered by the court, and a copy of the divorce decree and orders implementing the decree. MHS holds pre-1950 civil case files from a majority of Minnesota counties. Case numbers can be found in the plaintiffs and defendants indexes and/or in the registers of civil actions series in the district court records. Most of these series remain in the custody of the district court administrator in each county, although an increasing number of them are being transferred to MHS. A copy of the final divorce decree will usually be found in the district court judgment book (frequently called judgment record) series. MHS holds judgment books for most Minnesota counties until about 1982.

Election and Appointment Records

See also Municipal Records; School Resources: County Superintendent of Schools Records, Public School District Records; Township Records

Bond and Oath Records (Elected and Appointed)

Elected and appointed officials of state and local governments post bonds and swear oaths to ensure that they will carry out the responsibilities of their offices. The records usually include name of officer, office to which elected or appointed, effective date and term of appointment, and name of bondholder. The records of the territorial secretary include oaths and bonds for territorial and local offices, 1849–57. The records of the secretary of state, beginning in 1858, include oaths and bonds of elected state officials, appointees to statewide official posts, appointees to boards and commissions, and appointees to such offices as game warden and state inspector; they also contain registers of oaths and bonds of county officials, 1875–1914. Oaths and bonds of local officials (including officers of counties, cities, villages, townships, and school districts) are found in the records of the respective district court, county auditor, and county register of deeds (recorder). The statutes governing filing requirements for officeholders have varied significantly over time.

Note: These records may be titled differently from county to county; occasionally, they are listed within the respective district court registration records. Some records are indexed.

Election Records

Affidavits of nomination, campaign expense statements with indexes to filings, election-contest records, abstracts of votes, and nominating petitions. These may give names of candidates, vote totals, office, campaign donations, and expense statements. Researchers will find many Minnesota residents, especially in rural areas, who ran for municipal, township, and school offices.

Note: The records are arranged chronologically by election year, then by election (primary, general, and special). Election returns for 1858–1962 are microfilmed (SAM 66); available for sale and interlibrary loan.

Voter Records

Lists of registered voters and lists of individuals who voted appear irregularly in municipal, township, school district, and county records. Usually, these lists contain no more than the individuals' names or signatures. A particularly rich series of register of electors for the city of

Minneapolis is available on microfilm for the years 1902 to 1923. Each entry gives the voter's name and address; whether or not they voted in a primary or general election; birthplace; color, sex; length of residence in the United States, Minnesota, and election district; and naturalization date and place.

Note: The Minneapolis register of electors microfilm (SAM 104) is available for sale and interlibrary loan.

Ethnic Group Resources

Minnesotans can trace their families and their state's heritage to a multitude of ethnic groups. For detailed information about more than 60 groups that have lived in the state, see *They Chose Minnesota: A Survey of the State's Ethnic Groups,* edited by June Drenning Holmquist (St. Paul: Minnesota Historical Society Press, 1981). Separate and concise books about some individual ethnic groups appear in The People of Minnesota series, including such volumes as *African Americans in Minnesota* by David Vassar Taylor (Minnesota Historical Society Press, 2002), *Germans in Minnesota* by Kathleen Neils Conzen (2003) and *Chinese in Minnesota* by Sherri Gebert Fuller (2004). The MHS collections contain a wealth of materials about various ethnic groups, which can be found by using the names of the group and the state (as in "Irish Americans Minnesota") to search the Library's on-line catalog (at http://www.mnhs.org/library/search/index.html) for published and manuscript items, and the Visual Resources Database (at http://collections.mnhs.org/visualresources) for photographs and portraits. The Library catalog also lists general histories of many ethnic groups, as well as guides to genealogical research focusing on specific groups.

Family Histories
See also Biographical Resources

MHS holds approximately 12,000 family histories published in a variety of forms: typed, printed, mimeographed, computer-generated, and standard publisher's format. Ranging from a few pages to 1,000 or more, the histories cover families throughout the United States with emphasis on New England and the Midwest.

The Russian-born Copilovich brothers and sisters of St. Paul pose about 1912. Left to right are (standing) Samuel (Hebrew name Shmuel Behr), Max, Jacob, Henry (who was village president of Hinckley, 1905–8), and (seated) Ida (Mrs. David Gingold), Sam (sometimes known as James, whose Hebrew name was Isaiah and who used the spelling Kopilovich), Sara (Mrs. Max Goldbarg), Gershon (also known as George, and a teacher in a Jewish school), and Molly (Mrs. A. B. Fink). The first to immigrate to Minnesota were Max and Henry; their parents remained in Russia.

Genealogical records collected by individual researchers may include ancestor charts, family group sheets, correspondence, photographs, maps, vital statistics, newspaper clippings, autobiographies, greeting cards, and family histories. The records may be originals, photocopies, or microfilms.

Farm Records
See also Disaster Relief Records; Public Service Department Records

Agricultural Census
A typical entry includes: name of owner, agent, or manager of farm; acres of land; cash value of farm; value of farming implements and machinery; number of livestock; produce during year; value of animals slaughtered. There are agricultural censuses for Minnesota for 1850, 1860, 1870, and 1880.

Note: Microfilm; available for sale and interlibrary loan.

Century Farm Applications
Applications to the State Agricultural Society from residents who wished to have their farms designated century farms, signifying that the farm had been in the same family for 100 or more years. The Minnesota State Fair and *Farmer* magazine initiated this joint project in 1976. The forms give biographical and genealogical information and ownership history of the farm, and some include reminiscences.

Note: The forms are filed first by year, then alphabetically by county.

Drought Relief Applications
Applications, 1933, with information about applicant's name; age; marital status; number at home in family; size of farm and terms of rental and/or mortgage status; value of personal property; livestock; auto; machinery; cash on hand; hay and grain in stock; debts; average monthly cream check; other income; number of bushels of corn, oats, barley; tons of hay; fuel for farm equipment; and other commodities being requested.

Note: The records are arranged by county (a county with a large number of applicants may be subdivided by township).

Farm Crop and Labor Reports

Reports include name of farmer, address, nearest shipping point, name of railroad, nationality or descent of farmer, kind of crops and acres planted in 1917 and 1918, livestock and number of each kind, number of silos, and report of farm labor needs. Individual reports are not extant for all counties.

Note: Microfilm (SAM 217); available for sale and interlibrary loan. The records are not indexed, but are arranged by county, then alphabetically by surname of farmer.

Hail Relief Applications

Applications, 1930–34, with information about applicant's name, age, marital status, number at home in family, size of farm, value of personal property, livestock, auto, machinery, cash on hand, hay and grain in stock, debts, average monthly cream check, other income, number of bushels of crops, fuel for farm equipment, and other commodities being requested. Records for 1930 are for Marshall County only.

Note: The records for 1931 are arranged by county; those for 1932 and 1933 are alphabetical by surname within each county.

Livestock Dealers Proceedings

The Railroad and Warehouse Commission was responsible for licensing and regulating livestock dealers and buyers for resale. The files, 1938–68, document complaints against individual dealers and include hearing transcripts and correspondence.

Plat Books

Maps and atlases that show land ownership by county and may include county histories, directories and biographies of farmers and landowners, urban plats, and photographs and other illustrations. This information was obtained from land ownership records in the offices of the county registers of deeds and from canvassings of the counties. Publication dates are irregular. The collection includes more than 500 county atlases for Minnesota from the 1860s to the present and about 200 county or state atlases from other parts of the country, mostly New England, the Midwest, North Dakota, and South Dakota.

County _Beltrami_   Township (City or Village) _Eckles_

Name _Julius Malawaski_ Post Office Address _Bemidji_ R. F. D. No. _1_

Nearest Shipping Point _Wilton_   What Railroads _G. N._

Nationality or descent of farmer _American_

FARM CROP AND LABOR REPORT

Crop	Acres in 1917	Acres in 1918
Barley		
Beans	1/8	
Beets		
Buckwheat		
Corn	1 1/2	
Fruit		
Hay	4	
Oats	8	
Potatoes	1/2	
Rutabagas	1/4	
Rye		
Spelts		
Sorghum		
Sugar Beets		
Wheat		

Stock	Number in 1917	Number in 1918
Hogs	2	1
Horses	2	2
Milch Cows	2	3
Other Cattle	2	2
Poultry	50	30
Sheep		

Silos now erected		
To be erected in 1918		

DO YOU NEED MORE FARM LABOR?	Men	Women	Boys
How many?	2		
When?	Sept		
For how long?	2 week		
For what work?	corn & ~~oats~~		
What nationality?			

Remarks: _____

The foregoing statement was made on the _6_ day of _May_ A. D. 1918.

Lw. Aldrich

Signature of Assessor.

This return is made to your County Auditor, and by him sent to J. A. O. Preus, State Auditor, State Capitol, St. Paul, Minn.

Note: Pre-1914 maps are on microfilm (MC 174, MC 175, MC 575); available for sale and interlibrary loan.

Rural Credit Department Records

The Rural Credit Department (1923–73) loaned money to farmers threatened by loss of their land during the Great Depression of the 1930s. Farmers were given the opportunity to repay loans slowly. The incomplete records in the State Archives include real estate loan records, loan record cards, sales journals, lease records, and contract for deed files. Genealogical information is limited to farm histories, correspondence regarding ownership, and financial information on the farm and its produce.

Stallion Registration Board Records

The Stallion Registration Board, authorized by the legislature in 1907, regulated the use of stallions for public service (mating of a stallion to the mare of another owner) by verifying their soundness and their breeding. The board registered draft horses exclusively. The board was dissolved in 1953. Records of genealogical interest consist of registration card files, 1910–1950s, which is an index to owners listing the owner's name and residence (as well as other information); and registry books, 1921–52, which include names of stallion and owner, residence, names of breeders and the examining veterinarian, and reference to certification by any other registry association.

Genealogical Organizations Publications

Periodicals and books published by the Minnesota Genealogical Society (MGS), genealogical organizations from around Minnesota, and the majority of the state genealogical organizations in the United States can all be found in the MHS collections. Of particular interest are MGS's periodical, *Minnesota Genealogist* (St. Paul: Minnesota Genealogical Society, 1970–), and *Minnesota Genealogical Journal* (Brooklyn Park, Minn.: Park Genealogical Book Co., 1984–). MGS also has published

LEFT: *Farm Crop and Labor Report form for Julius Malawaski, a farmer living near Bemidji in 1918*

several volumes of ancestor and family-group charts noting the ancestral lines of some of its members.

Governor's Office Records
See also Professional Certificates, Licenses, and Registrations

Appointment Records
Records of appointments to state boards, commissions, and departments; appointments of judges; and other appointments giving name of person, name of office, date of appointment, and expiration date.

Note: Indexes exist for 1898–1953 only.

Citizenship Restoration Records
Certificates sent to the governor, 1889–1963, by wardens, superintendents, officials, and judges affirming the rights of persons to restoration of citizenship following completion of prison or reformatory sentences, suspended sentences, or probation periods. The records may have name, date of conviction, nature of crime, date of sentence, in what court sentenced, and date of release.

Note: The records are arranged chronologically, then alphabetically for each type of certificate.

Pardon Records
Pardons requested of the governor or the pardon board by individuals convicted in Minnesota courts. The records may consist of applications detailing reasons for the pardon or commutation of sentence, letters or affidavits in support of or in opposition to the pardon, and administrative records relating to the request. Occasionally, a transcript of the original trial is included. Records in the State Archives include pardon application registers (1897–1934), pardon applications (1889–1980), and pardon calendars (1897–1954). Additional records, especially for the nineteenth century, can be found in the Governor's Office Records, particularly in the "Executive journals" and the "Records"—subject files and correspondence—of individual governors.

Health and Welfare Records
Child Welfare Survey Cards (Ramsey County)

An incomplete 1918 survey giving name, address, sex, place of birth, whether birth was registered, age, height, weight, pounds underweight, serious disease or defect, name of examiner, and notes on follow-up contacts.

Note: The survey is arranged by wards within the city of St. Paul. The records are not indexed.

Poor Farm Records

Most Minnesota counties operated poor farms. Some farms date from the 1860s—although most began later in the nineteenth century or early in the twentieth—and continued up to the 1950s. Some became nursing homes or tuberculosis sanatoriums, usually no longer operated by the county. Records of several poor farms are in county records in the State Archives. These usually contain registers of residents ("inmates" in the terminology of the time period) that give date and cause of application and some or all of the following information: applicant's name, nationality, marital status, age, birthplace, length of residency in state or county, occupation, health status, and death date. *A Historical Directory of Minnesota Homes for the Aged* by Ethel McClure (St. Paul: Minnesota Historical Society, 1968) may be useful in identifying records of poor farms and municipally owned nursing homes.

Private Hospitals/Facilities Records

Records of many private health and welfare institutions, about the institutions themselves and their patients. Examples of such collections are the records for Abbott Northwestern Hospital (Minneapolis), Fairview Deaconess Hospital School of Nursing (Minneapolis), Maternity Hospital of Minneapolis, Babies Home of St. Paul, and Edward F. Waite Neighborhood House (Minneapolis). The records contain administrative files governing the operations of the facility, and financial records. Although the MHS Library does not have individual patient case files, information about patients may be found in series such as admission and discharge registers and correspondence. Patient registers of Luther Hospital (St. Paul) and Ellsworth Hospital (Nobles

County) are in the records of the Minnesota Department of Health in the State Archives.

Note: Access to certain records may be restricted.

Public Hospitals/Facilities Records

See also Death Records: Cemetery Records; Military and Veterans' Records: Veterans' Facilities Records

The MHS collections contain records of state facilities for the care of the mentally retarded, mentally handicapped, chemically dependent, criminally insane, and physically handicapped. The facilities include the following state hospitals:

- Anoka State Hospital, opened in 1900
- Brainerd State Hospital, opened in 1958
- Cambridge State Hospital, operated 1925–97
- Faribault State School and Hospital, operated 1879–1998
- Fergus Falls State Hospital, opened in 1890, scheduled to close in 2004
- Gillette State Hospital for Crippled Children (St. Paul), opened in 1897
- Hastings State Hospital, operated 1900–1978
- Moose Lake State Hospital, operated 1938–95
- Rochester State Hospital, operated 1879–1982
- St. Peter State Hospital, opened in 1866
- Sandstone State Hospital, operated 1950–59
- Willmar State Hospital, opened in 1912.

MHS does not hold any medical case files from Minnesota state hospitals, except for Gillette State Hospital for Crippled Children for the years 1897–1916. The records MHS does hold vary from facility to facility, but may include admission and discharge registers; patient case books, primarily before 1900; hospital or clinic registers; birth and death records; cemetery records; autopsy reports; population reports; and, occasionally, commitment papers. Check the on-line catalog to see what is available for each hospital. Administrative records may include minutes, annual and biennial reports; executive correspondence, summary financial records; facility publications; and operating records. Non-resident (employee) records may include personnel and payroll records before 1940.

The State Archives also has records of former tuberculosis sanatoriums. Sanatorium records may contain admission and discharge registers, annual and biennial reports, financial records, and minutes of the governing authority. Occasionally, the records may include payrolls. Dates for MHS records holdings coincide with the dates of operation of the following sanatoriums:

- Minnesota Sanatorium for Consumptives (popularly known by the name of its post office, Ah-Gwah-Ching, located near Walker; name officially changed in 1957 to Minnesota State Sanatorium; operated from 1907–63; in 1961 the Hennepin County sanatorium at Glen Lake became the official state facility for tubercular patients and the facilities at Walker became the Ah-Gwah-Ching Nursing Home, a state institution for geriatric patients)
- Glen Lake Sanatorium (Minnetonka, operated as the Hennepin County tuberculosis hospital from 1916–61; in 1961 the program at Ah-Gwah-Ching in Walker merged with the program at Glen Lake and became the Glen Lake Sanatorium from 1916–91; also in 1961, the legislature established the Oak Terrace Nursing Home at the same site for use as a geriatric care program for patients discharged from the state mental hospitals).

Other sanatoriums operated by counties or groups of counties for which records about the patients (residents) are available include:

- Buena Vista Sanatorium (Wabasha; Winona and Wabasha Counties, 1917–55)
- Lake Julia Sanatorium (Beltrami County, 1916–48)
- Riverside Sanatorium (near Granite Falls; Chippewa, Lac qui Parle, Renville, and Yellow Medicine Counties, 1917–64; became Riverside Out Patient Clinic, 1964–73).

MHS has no patient (resident) records, but does have administrative records, for the following county sanatoriums:

- Nopeming Sanatorium (Nopeming; St. Louis County, 1912–71)
- Southwestern Minnesota Sanatorium (near Worthington; Cottonwood, Jackson, Lincoln, Lyon, Murray, Nobles, Pipestone, and Rock Counties, and joined later by Blue Earth, Le Sueur, Redwood, and Watonwan Counties, operated 1917–1957; several of the counties joined the Riverside Out Patient Clinic in Granite Falls)

• Sunnyrest Sanatorium (Crookston; Polk and Norman Counties, joined later by Marshall, Pennington, Red Lake, and Roseau Counties, operated 1916–67).

Note: Access to patient records is restricted for 50 years from the date of creation.

State Orphanage (Owatonna)

See also Adoption Records; School Resources: State Special Educational Facilities Records

The State Public School in Owatonna was established by the legislature in 1885 as an institution for dependent and neglected children between the ages of 3 and 14. Children were committed to the school by county commissioners after an investigation by the county probate judge; in 1917 the power of commitment was transferred to the county juvenile court. Efforts were made to place all children in adoptive homes. The practice of indentured placement, whereby children were put in homes (often farms) on contract to do work or learn a trade in exchange for a payment to the state, was used on a limited basis until it was abolished in 1936. Children who were not placed in homes were discharged when they became self-supporting or when their parents were able to care for them. The population of the school fluctuated between 200 and 400 from the turn of the century to 1945. The State Public School vacated the facilities at Owatonna in 1945 to allow a school for the mentally retarded to occupy the site; the State Public School was formally abolished in 1947.

The State Archives contains case files for 1886–1945 on individual children. Files for children who were under guardianship when the school closed in 1945 generally were not included in the files transferred to MHS, but went instead to the Department of Human Services. An index to the residents' records, also covering 1886–1945, is arranged in alphabetical order by surname. The index card includes the following information: name and case file number of student, date of admission, county of residence, date and place of birth, parents' names and residence, names of siblings, date placed and with whom, date adopted, date discharged (attained age of majority, returned to parents, returned to jurisdiction of county, died at institution).

Note: Access to both the case files and the card index is restricted:

Adoption records less than 100 years old are available with a court order; adoption records more than 100 years old are open to the public.

Immigration Records
Alien Registration Records
This February 1918 listing of all non-U.S. citizens in Minnesota, excluding most Germans, was conducted by order of the Minnesota Commission of Public Safety. The two-page form includes information about a person's place and date of birth, port of entry and date of arrival in the United States, occupation, names and ages of children, financial situation, and male relatives taking part in World War I. The collection has been indexed, and both the index and the forms are on microfilm

Note: Microfilm (SAM 169; indexed by SAM 169-I); available for sale and interlibrary loan.

Americanization Survey Cards (Ramsey County)
A 1918 survey of families in St. Paul with names of family members; ward, precinct, and block number; church; lodge; and newspaper subscriptions. The information about each person more than 16 years of age includes age, sex, country of birth, race or nationality, years in the United States, citizenship status, whether English is spoken or written, whether any other language is spoken or written, marital status, birthplaces of father and mother, where attending English classes, physical defects, and occupation. For each person younger than 16 the survey also includes information about last school and grade attended.

Note: Microfilm (SAM 220); available for sale and interlibrary loan. The cards are not indexed.

Naturalization Records
First papers (declaration of intention, petition, application, and registry) and final papers (oath, petition, and certificate) required for persons applying for U.S. citizenship. Records before 1906 include name, date of filing, present residence in state, previous residence by state or country, renunciation of former allegiance, oath of allegiance, and witnesses' names. The record may include the date and port of entry into the United States. A standard form established in 1906 required more

specific information about the person: personal description, names of wife and children, place of birth, place of residence, and date and location of entry into the United States.

From the earliest naturalizations in Minnesota, beginning in 1849, married women and children were not listed in naturalization papers. From 1906 to 1922, married women and children were listed on the husband/father's papers. In 1922 changes in federal law enabled a wife to obtain her own citizenship independent of her husband.

Note: There are printed and microfilm indexes for each county. Records for all counties are on microfilm and available for sale and interlibrary loan.

Passenger Ship Lists

MHS holds indexes to many printed passenger lists. MHS does not hold the original passenger lists. Since Minnesota was not a first port of arrival, there are no federal records of passengers arriving at Minnesota ports. Steamboats arriving in Minnesota were not required to deposit passenger lists with any governmental agency; however, some steamboat passenger arrivals are listed in newspapers published in the cities where the passengers debarked.

About 10 percent of the available passenger lists are indexed in *Passenger and Immigration Lists Index: A Guide to Published Arrival Records of About 500,000 Passengers Who Came to the United States and Canada in the Seventeenth, Eighteenth, and Nineteenth Centuries*, edited by P. William Filby (3 volumes, 18 supplements; Detroit, Mich.: Gale Research Co., 1981–). Many of the published books and periodical articles indexed in Filby's guide are available in the MHS Library. Other useful indexes include:

- *Germans to America: Lists of Passengers Arriving at U.S. Ports, 1850–1855*, edited by Ira A. Glazier and P. William Filby, series 1: 67 volumes (1988–2001); series 2: 4 volumes– (2002–) (Wilmington, Del.: Scholarly Resources)
- *The Famine Immigrants: Lists of Irish Immigrants Arriving at the Port of New York, 1846–1851*, edited by Ira A. Glazier and Michael Tepper (as-

RIGHT: *Final naturalization papers issued in Kittson County for Nils Brenberg, who renounced allegiance to the king of Norway and Sweden in 1885 and became a U.S. citizen*

STATE OF MINNESOTA,
COUNTY OF KITTSON.
}

DISTRICT COURT.
11th Judicial District.

Special June Term, 188*5*

In the matter of the application of *Nils Brenberg* to become a Citizen of the United States, *Ed. Westerson* and *M. Mattson*

being severally sworn, do depose and say, each for himself, that he is well acquainted with the above named *Nils Brenberg* that he has resided within the limits and under the jurisdiction of the United States for five years last past, and for one year last past within the State of Minnesota; and that during the same period he has behaved himself as a man of good moral character, attached to the principles of the Constitution of the United States, and well disposed to the good order and happiness of the same.

Subscribed and sworn to in open Court, this _24th_
day of _June_ 188*5*
W F Wallace Clerk.

Ed. Westerson
M. Mattson
his
Mark
John Paulson witness

STATE OF MINNESOTA,
COUNTY OF KITTSON.
}

DISTRICT COURT,
11th Judicial District.

I, *Nils Brenberg* do swear that I will support the Constitution of the UNITED STATES OF AMERICA, and that I do absolutely and entirely Renounce and Abjure forever, all Allegiance and Fidelity to every Foreign Power, Prince, Potentate, State or Sovereignty whatever; and particularly to the *King* of *Norway & Sweden* whose subject I was; and that I have resided within the United States for five years last past, and in this State for one year last past.

Subscribed and sworn to in open Court, this _24th_
day of _June_ 188*5*
W F Wallace Clerk.

Nils Brenberg

STATE OF MINNESOTA,
COUNTY OF KITTSON.
}

DISTRICT COURT,
11th Judicial District.

AND NOW, TO-WIT: At a Term of said Court, now being held at *Hallock* in and for the County of Kittson, in said State, upon the foregoing oath and affidavits, and upon further proof having been made by the filing of a certificate, that the said *Nils Brenberg* did, before the Clerk of *District* Court *Polk Co. Minn* the same being a Court of Record, having common law jurisdiction, make the requisite declaration of his intention to become a Citizen of the United States, and to renounce all other allegiance, as required by the laws of the United States:

It is ordered by the Court, That the said *Nils Brenberg* be, and is hereby admitted to be, A CITIZEN OF THE UNITED STATES.

By the Court:

W F Wallace Clerk.

sociate editor) (7 volumes; Baltimore: Genealogical Pub. Co., 1983–86)

* *Migration from the Russian Empire: Lists of Passengers Arriving at the Port of New York*, edited by Ira A. Glazier (6 volumes; Baltimore: Genealogical Pub. Co., 1995–97).

Land Records

See also Maps and Other Geographical Resources; Railroad Records; Tax and Assessment Records

The acquisition, sale, and management of Minnesota's trust fund, railroad grant, and related lands, as well as the federal survey of Minnesota and the initial transfer of title of public lands to the state or to private parties, are documented in large part in records in the State Archives. See also *A Guide to the Records of Minnesota's Public Lands* by Gregory Kinney and Lydia Lucas (St. Paul: Minnesota Historical Society, Division of Archives and Manuscripts, 1985).

Deed Records

Records of the sale and mortgage of real property (land) are filed in the office of the county recorder (formerly register of deeds). The State Archives does not hold original county deed and mortgage records. Microfilm of such records, however, has been acquired for some counties (Brown, Carver, Dodge, Faribault, Itasca, Kandiyohi, Martin, Wadena, Waseca, and Washington, as of 2003) either from the county or from the Genealogical Society of Utah. Microfilm may include the actual deed or mortgage documents. Indexes exist for Hennepin County, arranged by grantee (buyer) or grantor (seller); for Olmsted County, there are registers containing chronologically arranged records of transactions.

Note: GSU microfilm is available for interlibrary loan.

Land Patent Records

Some key records, notably U.S. General Land Office land patent records, are located in the Bureau of Land Management, Eastern States Office, Springfield, Virginia. The Bureau of Land Management, General Land

Office's Official Federal Land Patent Records Automation website is located at http://www.glorecords.blm.gov/.

Original Entry Tract Books (GLO)

Books created by the U.S. General Land Office and later transferred to state custody, these items provide a consolidated record of the initial transfer of title from the United States to private parties or to the state, regardless of how the land was acquired (by homestead, preemption, scrip, or grant). For each parcel of land, the following information is recorded: price, original purchaser or transferee, number of the homestead certificate or other authorizing document, sale date, date the final patent (title) was issued, name of patentee, and citation to the entry in the land patent records in the U.S. General Land Office records in the National Archives. Land transfers are recorded by range and township.

Note: Microfilm (SAM 46); available for sale and interlibrary loan. An index organized by range and township can help researchers locate information about specific land parcels in the tract books. Both the tract books and the index (on roll 1) are on microfilm.

Register of Land Entries (GLO)

Records of the U.S. General Land Office districts documenting the acquisition of state land by cash purchase, various types of scrip, military bounty land warrants, under the provisions of the Homestead Act or Timber Culture Act, or of ceded Indian lands. These records may be variously titled Register of Entries, Register of Certificates to Purchasers, Register of Homestead Entries, Register of Final Homestead Certificates, Register of Military Bounty Land Warrant Entries, or Serial Registers. Although these records focus on the details of a land transaction, they also place the purchaser in a specific place at a specific time. Some contain brief personal information about the purchaser. Additional biographical information may be found among the registrars' and receivers' correspondence of the land districts, especially when the validity of the entries was contested.

Note: Search the on-line catalog by General Land Office district, or by the name of the specific land district if known, or by type of record if known (e.g., homestead record, contest docket).

Local and County Histories

See also Work Projects Administration (WPA) Resources

Annals of Minnesota (Federal Writers' Project)

During the late 1930s and early 1940s, the federal Work Projects Administration (WPA) gathered information on local history and wrote county histories. Information was gathered from newspapers and filed by name of county.

Note: Microfilm (M529); available for sale and interlibrary loan.

Manuscript Histories

Manuscript histories generally written by residents, telling the history of a community or county. May include interviews with early settlers, photographs, cemetery transcriptions, and listings of town and/or county officials.

Published Histories

Published histories constitute the most extensive of the MHS collection of materials about Minnesota's counties, cities, villages, and townships. Many were published before 1920 or as part of the celebration of the U.S. Bicentennial in 1976. Significant holdings of local history materials are available for the Midwest and for the New England states. The histories vary in scope, period of time, and quality.

Maps and Other Geographical Resources

See also Directories: Rural Directories; Land Records

MHS holds a collection of about 37,000 individual maps and 1,600 atlases. The emphasis is on Minnesota and the Midwest, but with selected reference maps and atlases for a wider geographical area. A major part of the collection is comprised of publicly and privately published, individual maps of Minnesota Territory and the state of Minnesota and its regions, counties, and cities. Although they are fairly general, these maps show the development of the area's political boundaries and transportation network, along with the spread of both urban and rural settlement. Of particular use to genealogists are the locations of many cities, towns, and villages that no longer exist and can be found only in gazetteers and place-name guides.

Fire Insurance Maps

Fire insurance maps and urban atlases for large urban areas, cities, towns, and villages. The atlases for Minneapolis, St. Paul, and Duluth (from the mid-1880s to the 1940s) cover the totality of the corporate limits, show most structures (including residences, industrial sites, and commercial buildings), and give legal descriptions of lots and blocks, with some building numbers.

Insurance maps and atlases of more than 950 Minnesota towns and cities provide—for built-up areas of a city—a "footprint" of a building and include information about building location and address, building material, function of building, number of stories, porches, outbuildings, and identification as a private dwelling or a rental property. Commercial designations, such as saloon or law office, are indicated, and schools, churches, and halls are identified. Publication dates range from the mid-1870s to the 1970s. Insurance maps and atlases of the Sanborn Map Publishing Company and the Rascher Insurance Map Publishing Company are available on microfilm for research and copying.

Gazetteers

Place-name guides for Minnesota, other states, and foreign countries. Entries may include original plat date, origin of name, and other historical information. The standard guide for Minnesota is *Minnesota Place Names: A Geographical Encyclopedia* by Warren Upham (3rd edition, revised and enlarged; St Paul: Minnesota Historical Society Press, 2001). An on-line version of *Minnesota Place Names* can be found at http://mnplaces.mnhs.org/upham/.

Plat Books

Maps and atlases that show land ownership by county and may include county histories, directories and biographies of farmers and landowners, urban plats, and photographs and other illustrations. This information was obtained from land ownership records in the offices of the county registers of deeds and from canvassings of the counties. Publication dates are irregular. The collection includes more than 500 county atlases for Minnesota from the 1860s to the present and about 200 county or state atlases from other parts of the country, mostly New England, the Midwest, North Dakota, and South Dakota.

Note: Pre-1914 maps of Minnesota counties are on microfilm (MC 174, MC 175, MC 575); available for sale and interlibrary loan. Copies cannot be made from plat books that are less than 25 years old.

Post Office Location Guides

The principal published list of post offices in Minnesota is *The Post Offices of Minnesota* by Alan H. Patera and John S. Gallagher (Burtonsville, Md.: Depot, 1978). The information for each post office includes the date of establishment and of discontinuance, if appropriate. The list is indexed by county and then by name of post office. A post office card file compiled by Newton D. Mereness notes any early changes of post office name and the name of first postmaster in each community. For the United States, the major guides are the *U.S. Official Register* (1831–1911) and the *U.S. Official Postal Guide* (1851–1978).

Note: Ask staff for assistance.

**United States Post Office Department,
Record of Appointment of Postmasters: Minnesota, 1832–1971**

Dates of establishment and discontinuance of post offices, their name changes, and the names and appointment dates of their postmasters. Beginning in 1870, it also gives the names of post offices to which mail from discontinued offices was sent. Alphabetical by county; thereunder by name of post office.

Note: Microfilm (M16).

**United States Post Office Department,
Reports of Site Locations: Minnesota, 1837–1950**

Includes location papers and supporting county, township, and city maps, some correspondence, and miscellaneous other records giving the locations of post offices, and proposed post offices, throughout Minnesota from the earliest days of white settlement to the mid-twentieth century. Location records are largely questionnaires to local and prospective postmasters and contain information on locations of local post offices and mail routes, frequency of delivery, names of carriers, information on the transportation infrastructure, and population data.

Note: Microfilm (M546).

Topographic Maps

Federally produced topographic map set of Minnesota in detailed scale. More than 1,700 sheets cover the state. Most were produced after World War II and contain information about the physical lay of the land and such cultural features as individual farms, small villages and towns, rural churches, and cemetery locations. They are often the only street maps available for many urban places. Many of the names on these maps are those in local usage, and often their sources are previously published maps and historical publications. Therefore, many names remain on the maps long after they have disappeared as functional places.

Note: Ask staff for assistance.

Township Organization Records

See also Township Records

Record books and files giving information about the organization of Minnesota townships and villages, including names, name changes, locations (legal descriptions), and dates and nature of changes in name, boundaries, or organizational status.

Ward Maps

Available for major cities, such as St. Paul, Minneapolis, Duluth, Rochester, and Winona. Wards changed over time, but these maps are still very useful when researching in the un-indexed census records of these cities.

Note: Ask staff for assistance.

Marriage Records

See also Church and Religious Organizations Resources

Marriage records in Minnesota vary in form and content depending on the time period and the jurisdiction in which the marriage was recorded. Marriages have been recorded in Minnesota counties since the organization of the counties. The records may consist of an application for license to marry, a license issued by the clerk of district court giving permission for an authorized officiant (usually member of the clergy, justice of the peace, or judge) to solemnize a marriage, and a return or certificate from the officiant noting that a marriage had been solemnized. Records generally include the names and residence (by county) of the bride and groom, occasionally their respective ages, the date of the application and license, and the date the marriage occurred, along with the place of marriage, name of officiant, and, if a member of the clergy, where the officiating clergy's credentials were filed. Most marriage records are indexed in some manner, although early records may be indexed only by the bridegroom's name.

Most Minnesota marriage records remain in the custody of the county in which the marriage was solemnized. MHS, in an arrangement with the Genealogical Society of Utah, is currently filming marriage records from Minnesota counties. The project is far from completion, and as of 2003 only a few counties have been filmed. As the microfilming is finished in a county, it will be added to the on-line catalog. (*Note:* GSU microfilm is available for interlibrary loan.) See table on pages 95–99.

The State Archives also holds a series of original territorial marriage records (1843–49, 1858) from territorial St. Croix County, Wisconsin, for marriages that occurred in areas east of the Mississippi River, including area that later became Minnesota.

Nineteenth-century marriage records from some of Minnesota's counties have been published in local and state genealogical journals.

Military and Veterans' Records
Published Materials
General Histories

The MHS Library has many general histories of various wars. For more information on Civil War sources see *Resources for Civil War History at the Minnesota Historical Society* by Hampton Smith (St. Paul: Minnesota Historical Society, 1998), or use this resource on-line at http://www.mnhs.org/library/tips/civilwar/civilwar.html.

Pension Indexes

The MHS Library has many published indexes to military pension files, including:

RIGHT: *Anoka County marriage record for Isaiah Gardner and Alice Dougherty, who wed in 1886*

STATE OF MINNESOTA, } *ss.*

District Court for the County of Anoka.

To any Person Lawfully Authorized to Solemnize Marriages within said State:

KNOW YE, *That License is hereby granted to join together as Husband and Wife,* Isaiah Gardner *of the County of* Anoka

and State of Minnesota *and* Alice Dougherty

of the County of Anoka and State of Minnesota, being satisfied by the Oath

of said Gardner

that there is no legal impediment thereto.

THEREFORE, *This shall be your sufficient authority for solemnizing the Marriage of said parties, and making return thereof as provided by law.*

In Testimony Whereof, I have hereunto set my hand and affixed the seal of said District Court, at Anoka, this 22nd *day of* Decr *188*6

L. S. Browning *Clerk.*

District Court

STATE OF MINNESOTA, }
COUNTY OF ANOKA.

I HEREBY CERTIFY, *That on the* 22nd *day of* December *in the year of our Lord one thousand eight hundred and eighty* Six *at* Anoka *in said County, I, the undersigned, a* Baptist Minister *did join in the holy bonds of Matrimony, according to the laws of this State,* Isaiah Gardner *of the County of* Anoka *and State of* Minnesota *and* Alice Dougherty *of the County of* Anoka *and State of* Minnesota *in presence of*

Newman Cochran
Mary J. Cochran } *Witnesses.*

John Mitchell

A COPY of my credentials of Ordination is recorded in the Clerk's office of the District Court for the County of _____ *in the State of Minnesota.*

Filed for record this 11th *day of* January *A. D. 188*7

L. S. Browning *Clerk.*

- *Index of Revolutionary War Pension Applications* (Washington, D.C.: National Genealogical Society, 1966)
- *Index to Old Wars Pension Files: 1815–1926*, transcribed by Virgil D. White (2 volumes; Waynesboro, Tenn.: National Historical Publishing Co., 1987)
- *Letter from the Secretary of War Transmitting a Report of the Names, Rank, and Line, of Every Person Placed on the Pension List, in Pursuance of the Act of the 18th March, 1818* (U.S. War Department; reprint, Baltimore: Southern Book Co., 1955)
- *Report from the Secretary of War . . . in Relation to the Pension Establishment of the United States* (U.S. Senate, 23rd Congress, 1st session, 1835, S. Doc. 514, Serials 249–51)
- *A General Index to a Census of Pensioners for Revolutionary or Military Service, 1840*, prepared by the Genealogical Society of the Church of Jesus Christ of Latter-Day Saints (Baltimore: Genealogical Pub. Co., 1965)
- *List of Pensioners on the Roll: January 1, 1883* (U.S. Senate, 47th Congress, 2nd session, 1882–1883, S. Doc. 84, Serials 2078–82; pensioners with Minnesota addresses are listed in Serial 2081, pages 531–91).

Rosters

Rosters for the Revolutionary and Civil Wars comprise the bulk of the published military records held in the MHS Library, with a smaller number of items for the French and Indian Wars, the War of 1812, the Mexican-American War, the Spanish-American War, and World War I. In addition to published rosters, a special Civil War veterans file was compiled to augment the information about Minnesotans who served in Minnesota regiments and to identify those who served with other states before moving to Minnesota after the war. This information may include residence, death date, widow's name, pension file number, regiment, and company. Several examples are:

- *Annual Report of the Adjutant General of the State of Minnesota for the Year Ending December 1, 1866, and the Military Forces of the State from 1861 to 1866* (1866)
- *Minnesota in the Civil and Indian Wars, 1861–1865* by the Minnesota Board of Commissioners on Publication of History of Minnesota in the Civil and Indian Wars (2 volumes; St. Paul: 1890–93)

• *Minnesota in the Spanish-American War and the Philippine Insurrection* by Franklin F. Holbrook (St. Paul: Minnesota War Records Commission, 1923).

Note: Ask staff for assistance. A limited number of the rosters are adequately indexed; the majority is arranged by regiment name or number and then by company. Rosters of men who served in Minnesota units during the Civil War and the Dakota Conflict of 1862 (also known as the Dakota War and the Sioux Uprising) are indexed.

Unpublished Materials
Manuscript Collections

The manuscript collections include many unpublished letters and diaries from men and women who served in the military from the time of the Mexican War through the Vietnam War. These records are cataloged in the on-line system and may be accessed by conflict, unit, or author. In the case of the Dakota Conflict of 1862, small collections of reminiscences and personal papers from many individuals have been gathered under one collection called the Dakota Conflict Manuscripts Collections.

Note: The Dakota Conflict Manuscripts Collections is on microfilm (M582); available for interlibrary loan.

State Archives Records

The records include bonus correspondence, daybooks, descriptive lists, hospital reports, inspection reports, lists of commissioned and non-commissioned officers, military appointments, military service record cards, monthly returns, muster rolls, payrolls and certificates of payments, pension information, orders, quartermasters' records, records of casualties, registers of men transferred, registers of men discharged, registers of deaths, registers of deserters, resignations and discharges, and miscellaneous information. The records include information for the Mexican-American War, the Civil War, the Dakota Conflict of 1862 (also known as the Dakota War and the Sioux Uprising), the Indian wars, the Spanish-American War, the Mexican Border Service, World War I, the Minnesota Home Guard, the Minnesota State Militia, and the Minnesota National Guard. Records may give person's hair and eye color, height, weight, place of birth, service unit, and ranking.

Note: Ask staff for assistance. Most records are not indexed, and many are in poor physical condition.

MILITARY SERVICE RECORD CARDS

Microfilm of service record cards for persons who entered federal military service via the Minnesota State Militia and the Minnesota National Guard. The information recorded may include name, service number, where and when enrolled, age or birth date, birthplace, residence, dates and places of service, service unit, rank or rating, where and when discharged, and civilian occupation. Included are records for the Civil War, the Spanish-American War (all branches of service), World War I (all branches, including nurses), the State Militia, and the National Guard.

Note: Microfilm (SAM 1); available for sale and interlibrary loan. The records are grouped by war and service branch, then alphabetically by surname within each group.

MUSTER ROLLS

Individual serviceman's name, date and place of enlistment, physical characteristics, date and place of discharge, age, amount paid, clothes provided, and remarks. Muster rolls for the Civil and Spanish-American Wars are included, along with a few for World War I.

Note: The records are not indexed. They are fragile, and their availability is limited.

PENSION REGISTERS

Pension registers and indexes cover Minnesotans receiving pensions for military service, from about 1877 to 1949. The records list claimant's name, date of filing, address, military unit, information to support claim, action on claim. Widows or children of servicemen filed many of the applications.

WORLD WAR I DRAFT REGISTRATION LISTS

Copies of the original draft lists from the U.S. War Department. The lists have the names, addresses, and draft numbers of 540,000 Minnesota men registered under the draft.

Note: The records are arranged by county and local draft board. They are not indexed and are difficult to read.

WORLD WAR I INDUCTION LISTS

Photostatic copies of the original induction lists, covering about 60 percent of the 80,000 Minnesota men called into service under the draft. The information includes induction number, name, date ordered to report, date and hour person reported, date forwarded to and reported at mobilization camp, date if failed to report at mobilization camp, date rejected, and date of final acceptance.

Note: The records are arranged by county, local draft board, and date. They are not indexed and are difficult to read.

WORLD WAR I MILITARY RECORDS

Biographical information and military service records for Minnesota men and women who served in World War I. The World War I Military Service Record, a four-page form voluntarily compiled by the individual, gives biographical information and military service record, including occupation before entry into the military and activities upon return to civilian life. The Gold Star Roll Record, a four-page form voluntarily compiled by family members, gives biographical information and military service records for men and women who died in service, including occupation before entry into the military, and information about date, place, and cause of death. Many of the forms contain a photograph and correspondence.

Note: Alphabetical arrangement. An index for the Gold Star Roll Record is available in the inventory in the MHS Library.

WORLD WAR II MILITARY RECORDS

Records of military service, for about 1941 to 1947, for men who were commissioned, enlisted, or inducted into the armed services during World War II. Information includes name, address, local draft board number, register number, date and place of birth, race, branch of armed services, dates of entry into and separation from the armed services. As of 2003, MHS holds records for Rice, Waseca, and Watonwan Counties and local draft boards number 14–25 of Hennepin County, covering northeast, north, and south Minneapolis, and some western and northwestern suburban areas.

Note: Search the on-line catalog by Hennepin County, Selective Service Record Cards, arrangement by board number, then alphabetical with each local board; Rice County, War History Committee, alpha-

6-14-21

STATE OF MINNESOTA
THE GOLD STAR ROLL

Compiled by the Minnesota Commission of Public Safety, co-operating with the Minnesota War Records Commission, to commemorate Minnesota men and women who made the supreme sacrifice while serving their country in the World War.

Name in full __Bast__ __Henry__ __A.__
(last name) (first name) (middle name)

White, Colored, Indian, or Mongolian? __White__ Date of birth __May__ __10__ __1890__
(month) (day) (year)

Place of birth __Galena Township, Martin__ __Minnesota__ __U.S.__
(town (county) (state) (country)

Residence prior to service __Fox Lake Tp., P.O.,Sherburn__ __Martin__ __Minnesota__
(town) (county) (state)

Parents (mark with X those deceased but give information requested)

Father: Name __Christ Bast__

Place of birth __Germany__

Residence __Sherburn__ __Martin__ __Minnesota__
(town) (county) (state)

Mother: Maiden name __Mary Sorg__

Place of birth __Germany__

Residence __Sherburn__ __Martin__ __Minnesota__
(town) (county) (state)

Wife: Maiden name __Single__

Place of birth

Residence
(town) (county) (state)

Gold Star Roll Record for Henry A. Bast from Sherburn, who died of influenza and pneumonia in a hospital in Le Mans, France, on October 6, 1918, while serving in the U.S. Army during World War I

betical arrangement; Waseca County, War History Committee, alphabetical arrangement by surname; Watonwan County, Selective Service Board, alphabetical arrangement by first letter of surname. Researchers should check the on-line catalog periodically to determine if similar records have been received for other counties.

SOLDIER BONUS RECORDS

SPANISH-AMERICAN WAR Applications for relief submitted by Minnesota veterans, or the survivors of veterans, of the Spanish-American War, the Philippine Insurrection, and the China Relief Expedition. Application packets contain such documents as application forms, affidavits of service, medical reports describing injuries sustained during service, discharge papers, marriage and death certificates, and facilitative correspondence.

Note: These records are indexed in Adjutant General, Soldiers' Bonus Records (SAM 3, roll 1); which is available for sale and interlibrary loan.

WORLD WAR I Applications to receive bonus payments, made to the Soldiers' Bonus Board from Minnesota soldiers, marines, sailors, and medical personnel who served in 1917–18 during World War I and in 1918–24 during the occupation. A 51-question application form includes the veteran's name, place and date of birth, name and residence of closest relative, draft information, present residence and occupation, name of employer and business address, name and address of parents at time of enlistment, length of residence in Minnesota, and marital status. The files normally include a discharge certificate, evidence of the applicant's military service, and administrative correspondence.

The records are separated into approved and unapproved applications. The approved application files are arranged by warrant (check) number and are indexed on microfilm (SAM 3). The unapproved applications are filed by application number. The application number for an individual veteran may be found under the veteran's name in the four un-indexed volumes of the "Soldiers Bonus Fund Warrant Record, 1919–1924."

Note: The approved applications are indexed on microfilm (SAM 3), which is available for sale and interlibrary loan.

In addition, bonus claim cards, 1921–22, are reference cards for applicants for World War I military service bonuses whose initial applications were rejected or not acted on in a timely manner by the Soldiers' Bonus Board and who appealed the board's decision or inaction to the Soldiers' Bonus Board of Review. Each card gives applicant's name and address, date of appeal, date the claim was received from the bonus board, date and place of hearing, action taken by the board of review, and date the claim was returned to the bonus board.

Note: Microfilm (SAM 228); available for sale and interlibrary loan. Arranged alphabetically by surname.

WORLD WAR II Applications for military service bonus payments to Minnesota veterans who served in World War II. They include data on the applicant's military service, proof of residence, and proof of honorable discharge (usually a copy of the discharge certificate). The initial deadline for bonus applications was December 31, 1950, but it was extended to December 31, 1951, and then to December 3, 1953. A few claims are dated 1955, and apparently required sponsorship of special legislation by the veteran's legislator.

Note: Microfilm (SAM 232 and indexed on SAM 232-I); available for sale and interlibrary loan. The microfilm is difficult to read.

KOREAN WAR Applications for military service bonus payments to Minnesota veterans of the Korean War. Minnesota law authorized "adjusted compensation" (bonus payments) to Minnesota residents who served honorably in the U.S. armed forces for 30 consecutive days between June 27, 1950, and July 27, 1953.

Note: Microfilm (SAM 158 and indexed on SAM 158-I); available for sale and interlibrary loan. The microfilm is difficult to read.

Korean War Bonus Beneficiary Records are applications for military service bonus payments to beneficiaries (members of the immediate family) of deceased Minnesota veterans of the Korean War. Minnesota statute defines who was eligible for compensation as a beneficiary.

Note: Microfilm (SAM 159); available for sale and interlibrary loan. The microfilm is difficult to read.

VIETNAM WAR Applications for military service bonus payments to Minnesota veterans of the Vietnam War. Minnesota law authorized bonus payments to Minnesota Vietnam War veterans, to be administered by the commissioner of veterans affairs. The law defined who was considered a veteran; established adjusted compensation in varying amounts up to $1,000, depending on type and circumstances of service; and required that applications for compensation be submitted by December 31, 1976.

Note: Microfilm (SAM 161); available for sale and interlibrary loan. The microfilm is difficult to read.

Vietnam War Bonus Beneficiary Records are applications for military service bonus payments to beneficiaries (members of the immediate family) of deceased Minnesota veterans of the Vietnam War. Minnesota statute defines who was eligible for compensation as a beneficiary. Applications include military casualty reports or death certificates, birth certificates, and marriage records.

Note: Microfilm (SAM 162); available for sale and interlibrary loan. The microfilm is difficult to read.

Veterans' Records

Veterans' Facilities Records

See also Health and Welfare Records: Public Hospitals/Facilities Records

MHS has resident and administration records for the state-operated Minnesota Veterans Home in Minneapolis (established in 1887), including admission and discharge records, histories of residents' military service, hospital and clinic records, and population reports. Administration records document the governance and operation of the veterans' home; they include minutes, annual and biennial reports, superintendent's correspondence, and summary financial records. Nonresident records include pre-1940 personnel and payroll records.

Note: Access to certain records may be restricted.

Veterans' Graves Registrations

Records maintained by the Department of Veterans Affairs describing branch of service, unit, cause of death, place of burial, and other biographical information. The records were compiled from 1930 to 1975. Records are arranged by county and chronologically with a separate section for Fort Snelling National Cemetery.

Note: The collection is indexed; ask staff for assistance.

Veterans' Organizations Records

Information about members of service units and activities, residences

State of Minnesota
DEPARTMENT OF VETERANS' AFFAIRS
400 Shubert Building
ST. PAUL 2, MINNESOTA
VETERANS' GRAVES REGISTRATION REPORT

Date June 3, 1949.

Full name of veteran ___ KNOWLTON, ___ Burton ___ Odell
          (Last Name)   (First Name)   (Middle Name)

Date and place of enlistment ___ 6-7-1942 ___ Omaha, Nebr.

Rank and organization ___ 648 37 45 ___ Aviation Machinist's Mate 2nd.C., ___ USN
                (Serial Number)   (Rank)   (Organization)

Date and place of discharge ___ October 31, 1945. Per. Sep. Center, Minneapolis, Minn.

Legal address or usual residence ___ Luverne, Minnesota.

Date of birth ___ 5-24,1921 ___ Place of birth ___ Luverne ___ Rock ___ Minnesota
                                    (City)   (County)   (State)

Date of death June 1, 1949. ___ Place of death Sioux Falls ___ Minnehaha ___ So.Dak.
                                  (City)   (County)   (State)

Cause of death ___ Bulbar Polio.

Next of kin ___ Marian L. Knowlton. ___ Wife
                (Name)   (Relationship)

Address of next of kin ___ Luverne, Minnesota.

Place of burial ___ Luverne ___ Rock ___ Date ___ June 3, 1949.
                  (City)   (County)

Name of cemetery ___ Maplewood ___ Grave location ___ N.E. 1/4 of lot # 137
                                        4th. Div. east.

L. R. Brinkman
(Signature of Funeral Director)

324 West Main St.,
(Address — number and street)

Luverne, ___ Minnesota.
(City)   (State)

INSTRUCTIONS

Complete this form in duplicate and forward both copies to the Department of Veterans Affairs, St. Paul 2, Minnesota, immediately after burial.

[stamp: STATE OF MINNESOTA DEPARTMENT OF VETERANS' AFFAIRS JUN 6 1949 RECEIVED]

The 1949 burial in Luverne of Burton Odell Knowlton, who served in the U.S. Navy during World War II, is recorded in this Veterans' Graves Registration Report form.

of members since military service, and women's auxiliaries. The records may include applications for membership, obituaries of deceased members, biographical sketches, names and service records of members, personal narratives, reunion materials, and annual-meeting materials.

Note: The records are generally not indexed.

GRAND ARMY OF THE REPUBLIC (GAR) RECORDS

Central office files of the Minnesota Department of the GAR, an organization of men who served in the Union army and navy during the Civil War, plus records for many of the almost 200 individual posts established in the state between the 1880s and 1940s. Central office files include post charters and organizational records, departmental correspondence, membership information, encampment (reunion) files, and death reports (incomplete, 1889–1920) received from individual posts. The records of posts include minutes of meetings, registers of members, personal narratives, descriptive books detailing the war service of members, correspondence, and post financial records.

Annual reports of GAR encampments—complete for Minnesota, 1881–1947—with miscellaneous reports for other states and national encampments. The reports describe activities of member posts, list officers, and note deaths occurring during the year, giving name of person, date of death, residence, and post, with an occasional biographical sketch. Publications of the Ladies of the Grand Army of the Republic auxiliary are also available.

Selected post records, chosen for their genealogical significance, are also available on microfilm (SAM 422). These records include descriptive books (register of members), membership applications, and biographical data. Also on microfilm are post adjutants' reports, submitted regularly to departmental headquarters by each GAR post (SAM 421). The post adjutants' reports contain rosters of post officers, lists of new members mustered or admitted by transfer, and summary membership statistics. The new member lists give name, age, birthplace, occupation, data on entry into and discharge from Civil War service, length of service, and cause of discharge. They were submitted quarterly for 1880–90, semi-annually for 1891–1917, and annually thereafter.

Note: Microfilm (SAM 421 and SAM 422); available for interlibrary loan. The records are not indexed.

MILITARY ORDER OF THE LOYAL LEGION OF THE UNITED STATES (MOLLUS)

An organization formed after the Civil War for men who served as officers. Manuscript collections of the Minnesota Chapter include membership records and published memorials. The published collections include memorials from some other states.

Note: The records are not indexed.

Motor Vehicle and Driver's License Registration Records

The MHS collections include some motor vehicle-related records:

* register of motor vehicles (1909–14, 1921), which includes vehicle number and description, and owner's name and residence
* records of chauffeurs (1909–11), which include name, city and county of residence, and date of registration
* motorcycle registrations (1909–13), which include vehicle number and description, and owner's name with city and county of residence.
* Records after the time periods listed no longer exist.

Note: The records are not indexed.

Municipal Records

See also Birth Records; Death Records; Election and Appointment Records; Prison Records

MHS holds records for more than 400 of Minnesota's 854 municipalities. After 1975 all villages became known as cities by legislative mandate. "Municipality" is the formal title given to cities of all sizes. Sets of municipal records vary in their completeness both in date spans and in record types.

The records include such administrative information as city council minutes, annual reports, correspondence and subject files; financial records, including payroll registers and registers of receipts and disbursements; municipal court and justice of the peace dockets; cemetery records, including burial registers and lot owner records; police jail registers and registers of tramps lodged in jail; death records; scrapbooks and newsletters; and poll lists and election registers containing the names of persons who voted in elections. Notable among the latter are Minneapolis registers of electors for 1902–23, containing significant genealogical information. Some municipal records include information about the registration or licensing of saloonkeepers, peddlers, and others. Names of city council members appear in the minutes, and names of city officials and staff can be found in payroll registers and annual reports.

Note: Most municipal records are not indexed.

Newspapers

See also Church and Religious Organizations Resources; Obituaries

MHS holds the world's largest collection of daily and weekly Minnesota newspapers, as well as non-English-language, labor, ethnic, reservation (*The Progress* and *The Tomahawk*), legal, prison (the Minnesota State Prison's *Prison Mirror*), religious, political, school, and other special-interest papers published in the state. Since 1957 legal newspapers—those publishing or carrying legal notices—have been required to file copies with MHS. The completeness of an individual newspaper file varies with the city and the time period.

For information about the names, locations, and publishing histories of Minnesota newspapers, see:

- *Gale Directory of Publications and Broadcast Media* (Detroit, Mich.: Gale Research, 1990–)
- *American Newspapers, 1821–1936: A Union List*, edited by Winifred Gregory (New York: H. W. Wilson Co., 1937)
- *Newspapers on the Minnesota Frontier, 1849–1860* by George S. Hage (St. Paul: Minnesota Historical Society, 1967)
- *American Indian and Alaska Native Newspapers and Periodicals* by Daniel F. Littlefield Jr. and James W. Parins (Westport, Conn.: Greenwood Press, 1984–).

Note: Microfilms of many newspapers are available for sale and interlibrary loan. There is a master list of newspapers arranged by name of city and then title of newspaper. There also are separate lists for some of the special-interest newspapers. Combined, printed indexes are available for the following newspapers (here referred to by commonly known titles): the *Minnesota Pioneer* (1849–52); the *Minneapolis Star* and the *Minneapolis Tribune* (1971–80); the *Star Tribune* of Minneapolis (1981–86); the *St. Paul Pioneer Press* and the *St. Paul Dispatch* (1967–);

and the *Duluth Herald* and the *Duluth News Tribune* (1978–). Ask staff for assistance.

The Babcock Newspaper Index lists selected articles from early Minnesota newspapers, primarily of the 1849–59 period. Some of the subjects covered are travel, immigration, and the rise and decline of towns.

Note: Microfilm (M588); available for sale and interlibrary loan.

Obituaries

See also Biographical Resources: Biography Files; Death Records; Newspapers

Generally, small-town newspapers publish more detailed obituaries that may include the places and dates of birth and marriage, survivors, and biographical information. In larger cities, particularly Minneapolis and St. Paul, the older daily newspapers did not publish obituaries as they do today. If a death notice was printed, it was more often a notice of only the funeral. Researchers should be aware that obituaries were not found in only one section of the newspaper as they are today. There is no separate master index of obituaries published in Minnesota newspapers. The Biography Files in the MHS Library (see Biographical Resources: Biography Files) have many references to newspaper obituaries. Knowing the date and place of death will help to locate obituaries for persons not listed in the Biography Files.

Pioneer Settlers Obituaries and Index

Obituaries of Minnesota pioneer settlers collected by Edwin Clark, 1911–21. The obituaries were clipped from newspapers and pasted in a scrapbook. The scrapbook has been microfilmed.

Note: Microfilm (M598); available for sale and interlibrary loan. The microfilm contains an index with more than 2,000 entries.

Oral Histories

See also Church and Religious Organizations Resources

The MHS collections contain more than 1,500 oral history interviews with Minnesotans from all walks of life—from politicians and business leaders to farmers, labor leaders, and members of the state's major ethnic communities. Information about family life, holiday customs, im-

EMMET

Mr. and Mrs. Herman Friberg and children visited at E. Bakers Sunday.

Mr. and Mrs. Wm. Schemel and baby were Renville visitors Sunday.

Mrs. F. A. Sterns was a Renville visitor Monday.

Mr. and Mrs. Joe Klemia and children visited at John Prazak's Sunday.

Mrs. John Brummer and daughter attended the St. Johns Luth. Aid last Wednesday.

Louie Prazak visited with his friend Vernon Bratsch Sunday evening.

Aug. Dusterhoft visited at the Paul Dusterhoft home in Crooks Sunday afternoon.

Raymond Walker of Hector visited with his sister Mrs. Ed. Anderson Sunday.

Mr. and Mrs. B. Friberg of Iowa uncle of H. Friberg visited a few days at the later's home south of town last week.

CROOKS

Mrs. A. Hinderks spent Friday with J. J. Smith.

K. Dueth from Holland, Minn. is here looking after his farm.

at Hatton, N. D. on Friday.

Mr. and Mrs. Hans Agres, Mr. and Mrs. Albin Skalbeck drove to South St. Paul on Sunday.

Oscar Hanson and family of Hanley Falls spent the week end at Hans Rude's.

The Opdahl Ladies Aid meets Thursday, October 25 at Mrs. Ole Forkerud's. All welcome.

Mrs. Henry Baumen entertained the Merrifew Club on Monday evening.

Misses Olga Romness and Frank nurses at Monte hospital were in town on Sunday.

The villagers appreciate the services rendered by the Railroad men at the fire on Thursday.

Mr. and Mrs. Stener Helgeson, Mr. and Mrs. Elmer Roseberg of Minneapolis spent Sunday at Mrs. Thor Helgeson's.

Mrs. Lloyd Larson is here taking care of her mother's home during her absence. Mrs. B. G. Roste is in Minneapolis taking medical treatments.

The Hauge Aid meets Friday, Oct. 19 entertained by Mrs. Olaf Slattum. The Misses Slattum and Mrs. John Davidson. All welcome.

Married at the home of Mrs. Volding her son Julius and Mrs. Adolph Engen by Rev. Giere. They went to Minneapolis for a short visit.

The Trinity Aid meets Tuesday

A typical local-news section from the Renville Star Farmer of October 18, 1923, captures the current comings and goings and other everyday events in the lives of area residents.

migration, and community activities is represented, especially in the autobiographical reminiscences. Special projects document facets of the Asian, African American, Finnish, Jewish, Mexican, Scandinavian, labor, and church communities in Minnesota. Other projects focus on industrial and environmental history and on a major power line construction controversy in the 1970s. For a name, place, and subject index, see *The Oral History Collections of the Minnesota Historical Society*, compiled by Lila Johnson Goff and James E. Fogerty (St. Paul: Minnesota Historical Society Press, 1984), and the on-line catalog.

Note: Detailed information about each interview is available. Tapes for listening as well as many oral history transcriptions are available for use in the MHS Library. Access to certain interviews is restricted. Not all oral histories are in the on-line catalog; ask staff for assistance.

Organizations Records

MHS has information about members, residences of members, and activities of a variety of organizations: social, ethnic, fraternal, patriotic, and service-oriented. The records may include applications, biographical sketches, obituaries, organizational activities, and additional materials. Some records are in languages other than English.

Note: Records are not indexed.

The MHS Library also has a collection of publications by various types of organizations. Specific ethnic groups, such as the St. Andrew's Society (Scots); fraternal societies, which often grew out of insurance cooperatives, such as the Modern Woodmen of America; patriotic organizations, such as the Daughters of the American Revolution (DAR); religious organizations, such as the Knights of Columbus; and service organizations, such as Rotary International, are included.

The publications may be newsletters, annual reports, membership lists, histories, or constitutions and bylaws. They vary in format, frequency, and type of information included. Annual reports may have biographical information or obituaries of recently deceased members. Membership lists may also note addresses or death dates. Newsletters often mention mem-

RIGHT: *A page from an undated list of the St. Croix Valley Old Settlers' Association includes information about organization members, including name, place and date of birth, and date of arrival in Minnesota.*

St. Croix Valley Old Settlers.

Name	Origin	Born	Came	Place	Died	No.
Holden, N. S.		1822		Hudson	1884	115
Holmes, Wm.	N. Y.		1842		1886	48
Holt, Geo.	Ky.		1846			210
Holt, John	Ky.	1815	1845		1874	66
Hone, David	N. Y.	1808	1838		1887	27
Hooper, Wm. W.	Md.	1813	1843	Utah		64
Hospes, Adolph C.		1841	1854		1911	249
Howard, Robt.			1844			153
Hoyt, Otis	N. H.	1812	1848		1885	104
Hughes, Jas.	Va.	1805	1849		1873	112
Huit, John	Canada		1847		1873	96
Hungerford, Wm. S.	Conn.	1825	1838		1874	24
Hutchinson, S. Aug.	Maine				1880	126
Jackman, Henry A.	Maine	1819	1849		1889	110
Jackman, Mrs. H A	Maine	1829	1850	Mont.	1909	241
Jackson, Mrs Henry	N. Y.	1811	1842	Mankato	1894	258
Jewell, Gilman	N. H.		1847		1869	86
Jewell, Phil B.	N. H.	1816	1847		1898	186
Jones, Capt. J. W.					1850	154
Jones, Mrs Kate B.		1846	1847		1909	241
Jones, Sterling	N. Y.	1812	1850	Hudson	1874	133
Judd, Geo. B.	Ill.	1799	1839	Marine	1872	55
Judd, Lewis			1838	Ill.		27
Kattenberg, Chas.	Germany	1844	1848	Tay F.	1901	199
Kattenberg, Henry	Germany	1825	1848	Tay F.	1907	236
Kattenberg, Mrs Henry	"	1823	1848	Tay F.	1896	173
Kelsey, John	Maine	1830	1849	Tenn.	1864	186
Kennedy, Robt.			1844	St. P.	1890	40
Kent, Andrew	Scotland	1819	1850		1901	198
Kent, Jas.	N. Brun	1826	1849	Wis.	1878	111
Kent, Robt.	Scotland	1819	1840		1896	175
Kent, Thos.	N Bruns	1828	1849		1857	111
Kent, Capt. Wm.	N. B.	1824	1844		1904	223
Knowles, Eddington	Vy.	1821	1844		1863	59
Lacy, T.	Maine	1824	1854	Tay F.	1901	199
Lagroo, Jos.	Canada		1838		1861	21
Lammers, Mrs F. W.	Sweden	1834	1851	Stillw	1901	195
Lapointe, Antwine	Canada	1816	1840		1890	78
Laub, Fred R.			1849	S'Lou	1911	248
Lawrence, Phinneas			1840	Stillw	1847	31
Leach, Calvin F.	N. H.		1842	S'Louis	1853	46
Lennon, John G.	England		1848			100
Leonard, Chas E.	Mass.	1810	1847	St. P.	1890	84
Lichtner, Adam			1846			147
Livingstone, Alex			1845		1850	68
Lockwood, Wm. S.	N. Y.	1811	1842		1847	51
Loomis, David B.	Conn.	1817	1843		1897	178
Lowe, Chas. F.	N. H.			Fla.	1873	129
Lowell, Mrs. Wm.				Stillw.	1899	267

bers' activities. Publications of patriotic organizations often include all of the above as well as information about ancestors.

The Library has lineage books for the DAR, the Sons of the American Revolution, the Colonial Dames, the Ladies of the Grand Army of the Republic, the Mayflower Descendants, and other patriotic organizations.

Personal Papers

MHS holds hundreds of collections of personal papers, each of which may include correspondence, diaries, account books, reminiscences,

Entries for September 19 and 20, 1862, from the pocket diary of Samuel Bloomer of the First Minnesota Volunteer Infantry record Bloomer's suffering and the amputation of part of his right leg following the Battle of Antietam during the Civil War.

autograph albums, photographs, scrapbooks, and genealogies. At least one Minnesotan is always represented in each collection, but family and friends may be from elsewhere.

Note: Small collections of personal papers (one or two folders of papers) and reminiscences have been cataloged together in collection P939: Biographies.

Photographs

The MHS collections include more than 200,000 photographs of individuals and groups of people, locations, activities, and other aspects of life in Minnesota. Many of photographs can be researched on-line through the Visual Resources Database at http://collections.mnhs.org/visualresources. Numerous photographs can be viewed on-line; most can be viewed in person in the MHS Library. In addition to individual images cataloged in the database, there are photograph collections and albums listed in the on-line catalog; use the search term "pictorial works."

Community Photographs

Postcards, snapshots, news photos, and commercial studio photographs dating from 1850 to the present, taken in every Minnesota county and most towns. Photographs of the town where a person settled or grew up can be evocative when creating a family history. Occasionally, photographs may be found of the business or industry in which a person worked, or the school or place of worship attended. For St. Paul and Minneapolis, each photograph of a building is indexed by neighborhood and address, and house historians and neighborhood historians will find this very useful.

Minnesota Photographers Index

A database listing of photographers—from the 1850s to the present—compiled from city directories, business gazetteers, and other sources. The information includes name(s), address, and years of business. This index is of particular benefit in identifying a time frame for photographs that have a business label.

Note: Ask staff for assistance.

Shingobe, his wife, and their daughter, Susan Sam Razor, have a family portrait taken in Onamia about 1903–12. The beadwork on Shingobe's bandolier (or shoulder) bag features traditional Ojibwe floral designs.

Minnesota Photographers Vertical File

Folders of biographical information on photographers that amplify the notations in the Photographers Index.

Note: Ask staff for assistance.

Portraits

Individual portraits, from 1850 to the present. Occasionally, biographical information is attached to the photograph or its availability is noted. Each of the 1,400 formal portraits in the Lee Brothers Historical Photograph Collection has a biographical cover sheet.

Note: Search by name of person in the Visual Resources Database (at http://collections.mnhs.org/visualresources), the portrait card index, the St. Paul newspaper portraits index, and the Minneapolis newspaper portraits index.

Prison Records

See also Death Records: Cemetery Records; Municipal Records; Newspapers

MHS has prisoner records for the following years at these prisons/reformatories:

- Minnesota Home School for Girls (Sauk Centre), 1903–78
- Minnesota Security Hospital (St. Peter), 1911–24
- Minnesota State Prison (Stillwater), 1854–1978; see below for more information about this facility
- Minnesota State Reformatory for Men (St. Cloud), 1887–1978
- Minnesota State Reformatory for Women (Shakopee), 1919–77
- Minnesota State Training School for Boys (Red Wing), 1868–1963
- Willow River Camp, 1952–72.

Records vary from facility to facility, but may include inmate case files, admission and discharge registers, commitment papers, parole records, school records, inmate photographs, population reports, trial transcripts, hospital or clinic records, and disciplinary records. Administrative files documenting the operation of the facilities, including correspondence, minutes, annual and biennial reports, newsletters, and financial records also are found. "Non-inmate" records of genealogical interest include personnel and payroll records before 1940.

Note: Various indexes are available. Access to certain records is restricted.

Minnesota State Prison (Stillwater)

The premier set of prison records in the State Archives covers the Minnesota State Prison in Stillwater. Authorized by the territorial legislature in 1851, it received its first inmates in 1853, served as the primary incarceration facility for adult men and women until the opening of the Shakopee state reformatory for women in 1920, and continued into the late-twentieth century as the largest facility for adult male felons. Records in the Archives consist of discharged inmate case files (1890s–1978), commitment papers (1880–1978), transcripts of trials of inmates (1901–72), convict record books and inmate register sheets (1853–1978), and assorted physical condition, admission, discharge, medical, and parole records. In addition, Minnesota State Prison annual/biennial reports for 1861–84 list all prisoners and their offenses. The reports for 1860–73 list every person who was paid by the prison for supplies and repairs. Reports for 1853–1900 list the names of prison officials. These reports are particularly useful, since most published materials do not give names of inmates.

Note: Many records have restricted access; see staff for assistance. For an every-name index to Stillwater reports for 1853–1900, see *Minnesota Genealogical Index,* volume 1, compiled by Wiley R. Pope (St. Paul: Minnesota Family Trees, 1984).

Jail records for some cities and county sheriffs may include name, date of admission, date of discharge, and reason for admission. When searching for someone who disappeared during the Great Depression of the 1930s, try jail files. Itinerant persons looking for employment could often find temporary housing in local jails.

Professional Certificates, Licenses, and Registrations

See also Governor's Office Records

Persons who wish to practice various professions or trades in Minnesota have been required to register or to seek a state certificate or license. Licensing and regulatory board records and other materials in the State Archives give personal information about many examinees and licensees. Only some of the occupations are listed here. Published directories of practitioners, or annual or biennial reports of boards and agencies listing licensees are in the MHS Library; the material in Manuscripts Collections often contain additional information about persons in medicine, nursing, teaching, and other professions.

District Court Records

Registrations of practitioners of healing in the basic sciences (anatomy, bacteriology, chemistry, hygiene, pathology, and physiology), chiropody (podiatry), chiropractic medicine, dentistry, massage, medicine, optometry, osteopathy, and veterinary medicine, as well as notaries public. These practitioners are or have been required to register with the district court in the county in which they are practicing. The registrations may include records of training and other information. District courts also were required to accept credentials of ordinations from individuals licensed to perform marriages in the county.

Municipal Records

Information about peddlers, saloonkeepers, and other persons registering with, or seeking licenses from, municipal authorities. Such records appear occasionally in municipal records.

Professional Board Records

Records include licensing and other information about persons. The information varies according to the record group. Coverage dates, content, indexing, arrangement, and restrictions also vary. The dates given below indicate the earliest and the latest board records in the State Archives, but information about individual licensees may be present for only part of that time. More comprehensive information is in the State Archives notebooks in the MHS Library. The boards—and the years MHS has licensing records—include:

- Accountants: Minnesota State Board of Accountancy, 1909–70
- Barbers: Minnesota Board of Barber Examiners, 1897–1976
- Chiropractors: Minnesota State Board of Chiropractic Examiners, 1919–58

- Cosmetologists: Minnesota State Board of Cosmetology (formerly Minnesota State Board of Hairdressing and Beauty Culture Examiners), 1927–70
- Dentists: Minnesota State Board of Dental Examiners, 1885–1963
- Doctors: Minnesota Board of Medical Practice (formerly Board of Medical Examiners); 1883–1985 (photograph portraits affixed to most applications for 1906–28)
- Electricians: Minnesota State Board of Electricity, 1899–1967
- Healers: Minnesota State Board of Examiners in the Basic Sciences, 1927–74
- Lawyers: Minnesota State Board of Law Examiners, 1891–1921, 1944–58
- Masseurs: Minnesota State Board of Massage Examiners (duties transferred to the Board of Medical Examiners in 1929, and masseurs also were required to register with the clerk of district court in the county in which they practiced), 1927–74
- Nurses: Minnesota Board of Nursing, 1908–71
- Optometrists: Minnesota State Board of Optometry (formerly Minnesota State Board of Examiners in Optometry), 1913–39
- Osteopaths: Minnesota State Board of Medical Examiners in Osteopathy (formerly State Board of Osteopathic Examiners and Registration; board's responsibilities transferred to State Board of Medical Examiners in 1963), 1903–62
- Pharmacists: Minnesota Board of Pharmacy, 1885–1944
- Watchmakers: Minnesota Board of Examiners in Watchmaking, 1943–83.

Note: Indexes vary for each record group. Access to many records relating to health and legal professions is restricted; examination scores often are protected.

Other State Agency Records

Many state agencies have the authority to register, certify, license, regulate, inspect, or sanction persons and firms in various trades and services. Activities affecting human and animal life, as well as health, finances, and property, usually are covered. Agency records may contain application or certification information for individual persons. Among such records are those for the following:

Detective and Protective Agents
Registers of detective and protective agents for 1923–44 are in the governor's records and case files for 1945–69 are in the secretary of state's corporation division records, both in the State Archives.

Embalmers, Morticians, and Funeral Directors
Lists of embalmers, morticians, and funeral directors for the period 1898–1966 are in the Health Department's published records in the State Archives.

Health Care Professionals
Records for health care professionals for the 1870s–1980s are in the Health Department's published records in the State Archives.

Notaries Public
Notaries public are appointed and commissioned by the governor. Commissions must be recorded with the administrator of the district court in the county of appointment. Published lists of notaries public are available for various years in the annual and biennial reports of the secretary of state, 1861–1912, and in *Notaries Public in Minnesota* (Secretary of State, 1914–20).

Plumbers
Records of plumbers for 1935–75 are in the Health Department's published records in the State Archives.

Public Service Department Records
See also Business Records; Directories; Farm Records; Railroad Records

The Railroad and Warehouse Commission—and its successor after 1967, the Public Service Commission—had jurisdiction over telephone companies, public utilities, railroads—including the opening and closings of lines, service, stations, and line maintenance—bus companies, grain inspection, and regulation of street railways. Materials include complaint files, more than 200 telephone company annual reports, commission merchants licenses, index of more than 800 Minnesota railroad companies, and rail history files. Many of the annual reports include lists of members of the boards of directors and contain much information useful for local history. The Livestock Dealers Proceedings, 1938–68, include information on individual merchants.

Railroad Records
See also Business Records; Land Records; Public Service Department Records

Published Materials
Published materials include histories, timetables, annual reports, and newsletters issued by or about railroad companies and street and electric railways serving Minnesota. For company names, see:
- *Rails to the North Star* by Richard S. Prosser (Minneapolis: Dillon Press, 1966)
- *The Electric Railways of Minnesota* by Russell L. Olson (Hopkins, Minn.: Minnesota Transportation Museum, 1976) and its *Supplement* (1990)
- *Railroad Names: A Directory of Common Carrier Railroads Operating in the United States, 1826–1982*, compiled by William D. Edson (Potomac, Mich.: W. D. Edson, 1984).

Duluth, Missabe and Iron Range Railway Company (DM&IR)
Payroll records for the DM&IR and its two predecessor companies, the Duluth and Iron Range Railroad Company and the Duluth, Missabe and Northern Railway Company. The payrolls are organized by railroad, division and department, and payroll period. They contain the employee's name; job title; pay rate; compensation, including regular and overtime hours; and deductions. The records are fairly complete from 1884 through 1910. After 1910 there are records through 1970 for each year divisible by 10.

Note: Payrolls are on microfilm (M497); available for sale and interlibrary loan.

Great Northern Railway Company (GN)
Histories, correspondence, financial records, minutes, annual reports, newsletters, personnel files and indexes, and payrolls for GN. Before

the company records were donated to MHS, the majority of the personnel files were destroyed. MHS has employee file numbers 1–1587 and 1680–1927; some individual files are missing. A microfilm index (1890s–1900s) in rough alphabetical order gives the employee's name, job title, and employee number; it includes employee numbers 1 to about 383,000. Also on microfilm are annual reports (1880–1968) to GN stockholders.

Note: Microfilm (M379 is an index to the GN personnel files, and M247 is an index to the president's office subject files); available for sale and interlibrary loan. Also check the MHS website for a searchable on-line inventory that covers the entire collection.

The GN records include the un-indexed business records for more than 250 subsidiary companies. These may contain corporate histories, correspondence, financial records, minutes, annual reports, and payrolls. The payrolls usually give employee name and number, job title, pay rate, and hours worked during the pay period.

Northern Pacific Railway Company (NP)

Corporate histories, correspondence, financial records, minutes, annual reports, president's office subject files, and payrolls for NP. The payrolls usually give employee name and number, job title, pay rate, and hours worked during the pay period. Payrolls are by department or branch line and are not complete.

Note: Microfilm (M295 is an index to the president's office subject files); available for sale and interlibrary loan. Also check the MHS website for a searchable on-line inventory that covers the entire collection.

The employee personnel files 1–210,000 (started in 1909) may include employment application, age, nationality, birthplace, residence, medical-examination and accident reports, and records of promotions, leaves of absence, dismissals, resignations, suspensions, retirements, and deaths. The personnel files are arranged by employee number; many are missing. A microfilm index in rough alphabetical order gives employee name, number, and job title; it includes employee numbers 1 to about 303,000. Also on microfilm are annual reports (1870–1968) to NP stockholders.

Note: Microfilm: M380 is an index to the personnel files; available for sale and interlibrary loan. Also check the MHS website for a searchable on-line inventory that covers the entire collection.

A related source of information is the un-indexed daily record of new employees (4 volumes), listing new employees hired from 1909 through 1967. The register gives name, employee number, and hiring date. Another is the personnel reference file, which is an alphabetical list of selected employees (largely administrative and supervisory) with information about appointments, promotions, and other administrative actions.

The NP records include un-indexed business records for more than 200 subsidiary companies. These records may contain corporate histories, correspondence, financial records, minutes, annual reports, and payrolls. The payrolls usually give employee name and number, job title, pay rate, and hours worked during the pay period.

The records also contain un-indexed employee newsletters issued by individual departments or the advertising and publicity department.

Twin City Rapid Transit Company

Records of the company (and its subsidiaries and successors) that operated the streetcar and local bus system in the Minneapolis–St. Paul metropolitan area from 1891 until 1970. Included are employment records, payroll records, and employee retirement plan-pension records. The employment records include appointment record books, 1914–25; seniority record books, 1923–54; station seniority records, 1943–54; and employee appointment cards.

The appointment record books apparently pertain only to motormen, conductors, and bus drivers. They include the individual's name, appointment number, date, home station, position, and badge number. The seniority record books apparently pertain only to motormen, conductors, and bus drivers. They seem to be a record of discharges, resignations, retirements, transfers, leaves of absence granted, layoffs, vacation granted, sick leaves, etc., and are organized numerically by badge number.

The station seniority records pertain to women operators and conductors, and gives the individual's name, appointment date, appointment number, badge number, and final disposition. The employee appointment cards, arranged by employee surname, give the employee's name and address, badge number, appointment number, date employed, reason for leaving, last date in service, and station foreman's comments. Some also give employee's date of birth, whether married or single, etc.

Note: From the on-line catalog entry, researchers can access a searchable on-line inventory of all the records.

School Resources
See also Election and Appointment Records

College and University Resources
Records of a few colleges and universities held by MHS may include names of staff and students in various sets of minutes and student enrollment records. The collections may also include items published by a college or university, such as proceedings or minutes of faculty or advisory meetings, yearbooks, student magazines or newspapers, histories of the institution, and alumni lists.

Note: Access to some records may be restricted.

County Superintendent of Schools Records
Records providing countywide information about teachers and students. Until the office of superintendent of schools was abolished by the counties between 1950 and 1971, the superintendent received or compiled the following types of records containing genealogical information: teachers' annual or term reports, which include lists of pupils with ages, sex, and attendance records; school censuses, with information about school-age children and their families in the county; permanent pupil record cards, with comprehensive information about the student while he or she was in the district; lists of teachers, school officers, and other personnel; teacher examination and certification records; and teachers' insurance and retirement fund records. The records occasionally contain poll lists for school elections. Records are not complete for all counties, and there are none for some counties. Those records in MHS, however, usually cover several decades. Some series of records begin in the nineteenth century. The county superintendent of schools had ju-

risdiction over the rural (common) schools only, and the records generally do not include information on individual students for the graded and independent schools in the county.

Note: Access to some information is restricted.

Private School Records

Records of several private elementary and secondary schools. The records contain names of trustees, faculty and other personnel, alumni, and students in various sets of minutes, programs, directories, and newsletters.

Note: Access to some records is restricted.

Public School District Records

Records of approximately 3,000 rural and independent districts. The records vary greatly in their completeness, both in date spans and in types of records. Some of the school districts still exist today; others were consolidated as local districts were reorganized.

The records include clerk's and treasurer's financial records; school board minutes; pupil records; class records; teacher certification records; student and family censuses; class lists; school officer lists; records of auxiliary organizations, such as parent-teacher associations; records of teacher reading circles and various student clubs; library and textbook records; district consolidation records; records of school elections; and administrative records of several county superintendents of schools. Names of students appear in several record types and are found readily in the censuses, class lists, class records, and pupil records. Names of teachers are found in various teacher and student records, as well as in any financial records that contain payrolls. Names of school board members and officers can be found in the board minutes and financial records.

Note: Access to certain school records is restricted. Records are not indexed.

School Publications

Published works from about 35 Minnesota college-level institutions and 250 junior and senior high schools. Publications from colleges (state, private, and community-governed two- and four-year schools) include class bulletins, literary compilations, yearbooks, and histories. Year-books are the basic resource for secondary schools.

State Special Educational Facilities Records
See also Health and Welfare Records: State Orphanage (Owatonna)

Records of the Minnesota State Public School in Owatonna (1885–1947) for dependent and neglected children; the Minnesota School for the Deaf (now the Minnesota State Academy for the Deaf), organized in Faribault in 1858; and the Minnesota School for the Blind (now the Minnesota State Academy for the Blind), organized in Faribault in 1863. Records vary from facility to facility, but may include admission and discharge records, students' educational records, and population reports. Administrative records documenting the governance and operation of the facilities include minutes, annual and biennial reports, summary financial records, and operating records. Nonresident records include personnel and payroll records dated before 1940.

Note: Access to certain records is restricted.

Tax and Assessment Records
See also Land Records

The MHS collections include assessment rolls and tax lists for 55 counties. Assessment rolls for real property include the property owner's name; legal land description; building and land values used to provide estimated market value; classification and assessed value of each parcel of property. Assessment rolls for personal property include the property owner's name with assessed value for such items as livestock, jewelry, furniture, household and farm items, and other personal holdings. Tax lists include only summary financial information and indicate the actual amount of taxes paid on each person's real and personal property.

The records are usually in the Minnesota State Archives for the years 1901 and before, and for the years ending in 0 and 1 in the twentieth century through 1971. The records for the years ending in 2–9 may no longer exist. Individual counties may hold assessment rolls and tax lists not included in the MHS collections. Some sets are available only on

A county assessor's 1868 record book for Featherstone Township, Goodhue County, lists assessed value of real properties.

microfilm. The records are arranged chronologically, then alphabetically by political subdivision.

Note: Many sets are on microfilm and available for sale and interlibrary loan. See table on pages 95–99.

Teachers Retirement Association Records

MHS holds Teachers Insurance and Retirement Fund records for 1915–31. Included are annual reports submitted by the county superintendents of schools to the Teachers Retirement Association listing the name of each teacher, district number, total years teaching experience, number of years in district, number of months in session, number of months taught, annual salary, and retirement deduction. The records also include applications and affidavits for teachers working in publicly funded schools in 1915 and miscellaneous applications. Applications include teachers' work history before 1915. There is an incomplete and undated numerical and alphabetical index of teachers belonging to the fund.

Township Records

See also Election and Appointment Records; Maps and Other Geographical Resources: Township Organization Records

Records of about 750 townships, many dating from the organization of townships in the 1850s and 1860s. Clerk's and treasurer's books, board of audit minutes, annual meeting minutes, and road record books can be found in the MHS collections. Names of township officers and residents and their activities are available in these records. Residents' names also may be found in birth and death registers (ending 1953) maintained by the township clerk; burial permits; justice-of-the-peace docket books; chattel mortgage record books and indexes; real and personal property assessment books; land, road, and poll tax lists; warrant books; poll lists; and bounty records for wolves, trees, gophers, grasshoppers, and crows. Not all of these records are extant for each township. Access to birth records less than 100 years old is restricted.

Union Records

The MHS collections contain some union records, which may include union membership lists and dues paid and delinquent; lists of members accused of working for nonunion companies; requests for membership information; validations of membership; correspondence; meeting minutes; scrapbooks; election of officers; information about training programs. For example, the Cigar Makers' International Union, St. Paul Local, contains records of membership and payment of dues, as well as minutes about payment of sickness and death benefits. Records generally date from the 1880s through the 1970s.

Note: Access to some records may be restricted by donor.

Work Projects Administration (WPA) Resources

See also Church and Religious Organizations Resources; Death Records: Cemetery Records; Local and County Histories

During the late 1930s and early 1940s Minnesota WPA projects (sponsored by the federal government) produced a variety of published histories and manuscript materials, including information about church congregations, school districts, cemeteries, and other background research for county histories, some of which were never completed.

Annals of Minnesota (Federal Writers' Project)

Typed transcriptions of or excerpts from newspaper articles relating to the history of Minnesota, compiled (1938–42) from selected Minnesota newspapers. This manuscript collection's chronological files, subject files, and geographical files include information on broad topics such as counties, immigration and settlement, names, persons, and nationality (ethnic and racial) groups.

Note: Microfilm (M529); available for sale and interlibrary loan

Published Materials

Some of the information collected in Minnesota by the Historical Records Survey (HRS) of the WPA was published as *Inventory of the County Archives of Minnesota* (44 volumes; published 1937–42); *Directory of Churches and Religious Organization in Minnesota* (1942); *Guide to Church Vital Statistics Records in Minnesota: Baptisms, Marriages, Funerals* (1942); and *Guide to Public Vital Statistics Records in Minnesota* (1941). These publications describe the records available in county courthouses and individual churches as of about 1943, but do not duplicate the records themselves. Not all Minnesota county archives inventories were published. The MHS Library includes many similar HRS publications for other states. Additional printed materials about WPA projects include local history, but rarely mention specific persons.

Unpublished Materials

Background files for unpublished Minnesota county histories, including interviews with early settlers. Historical information on individual Minnesota churches and cemeteries gathered by WPA workers for possible publication. The box lists included within the inventories serve as indexes.

Handy List of Basic County Records
at the Minnesota Historical Society

MHS holds various records in original or duplicate form for each of the state's 87 counties. This table lists the records that are most requested by researchers. Regular researchers may want to check the MHS Library's on-line catalog (at http://www.mnhs.org/library/search/index.html) for additions and update the table as new records are added to the MHS collections.

Notes for table

* MHS has records for one or more townships and/or municipalities in the county but does not have countywide records. MHS also has statewide death cards for 1900–1907 and death records for 1908–96 that include information for this county.

** County seat and state capital

1. Many Minnesota counties were established at an early date but were not fully organized with elected officials and functioning offices until a later date. The established date is useful for census records; the fully organized date is useful for county government-created records. Some reference sources may list different dates because of name changes, boundary changes, or the difference between the organized date and the fully organized date. This table lists the fully organized date because it more closely corresponds to the date that a county began creating records. The established dates come from the 1999–2000 *Minnesota Legislative Manual*, comp. Secretary of State (St. Paul: State of Minnesota); the fully organized dates come from *Atlas of Historical County Boundaries: Minnesota,* ed. John H. Long and comp. Gordon DenBoer (New York: Charles Scribner's Sons, 2000).

2. Vital records are kept in the county courthouses, located in the county seats. Birth and death records usually begin about 1870 for counties formed by then. Marriage records usually begin about the time of the formation of the county. In 1908 the Minnesota Department of Health began keeping duplicate records of births and deaths.

3. Naturalization records may begin at the established date or earlier because of the difference between first papers and final papers.

4. MHS has birth records only to 1930, and an index to births to 1999 for Olmsted County.

5. MHS has marriage records only to 1951, and an index to marriages to 1984 for Olmsted County.

6. MHS has only city of Rochester assessment rolls for 1892–1920, and all of Olmsted County for only 1930–71.

7. MHS has only city of Rochester tax lists, plus two years, 1930 and 1931, for the village of Dover.

8. MHS has only personal property tax lists for Ramsey County.

9. MHS has an index to Sherburne County death records, 1870–1981, and an index to marriages, 1926–75, but no actual records.

10. The majority of Sherburne County wills are filed with the final decrees.

11. MHS has birth records for 1860–1930, and an index to births for 1870–1950 for Steele County.

12. MHS has marriage records for 1857–1920, and an index to marriages to 1982 for Waseca County.

13. MHS has death records for 1870–1940, and an index to deaths to 1982 for Waseca County.

14. MHS has tax lists for the city of Winona, 1878 and 1887, and for Winona Township, 1880.

COUNTY	COUNTY SEAT	YEAR COUNTY ESTABLISHED/ORGANIZED[1]	VITAL RECORDS[2]			NATURALIZATION RECORDS[3]	PROBATE RECORDS		TAX RECORDS	
			Birth Records	Marriage Records	Death Records		Final Decrees	Will Books	Assessment Rolls	Tax Lists
Aitkin	Aitkin	1857/1885	*		*	1870-1954	1878-1982	1884-1979	1920-51	
Anoka	Anoka	1857/1857	1870-1945	1858-1971	1870-1945	1855-1943	1879-1971	1860-1971	1857-1950	1930-61
Becker	Detroit Lakes	1858/1871	*		*	1872-1948	1872-1982	1883-1981		
Beltrami	Bemidji	1866/1897	*		*	1889-1956	1896-1982	1897-1981	1920-72	1876-1911, 1920-72
Benton	Foley	1849/1849	*		*	1846-1945	1850-1977	1852-1978	1850-1971	1860-1951
Big Stone	Ortonville	1862/1881	*		*	1860s-1954	1882-1984	1886-1984		1875-92
Blue Earth	Mankato	1853/1853	*		*	1850-1906	1890-1982	1858-1982	1862-1961	1863-1961
Brown	New Ulm	1855/1856	1870-1949	1857-1950	1870-1993	1850-1951	1857-1965	1858-1965		
Carlton	Carlton	1857/1871	*		*	1871-1952		1857-1982		
Carver	Chaska	1855/1856	*		*	1856-1943	1892-1978	1857-1982		1910-71
Cass	Walker	1851/1897	*		*	1872-1954	1897-1971	1900-1971		
Chippewa	Montevideo	1862/1870	*		*	1869-1955	1881-1982	1873-1982		
Chisago	Center City	1851/1852	*		*	1855-1954	1857-1963	1864-1962	1852-1941	
Clay	Moorhead	1862/1873	*	1872-1981	*	1872-1954	1872-1918	1872-1981	1930-71	1872-1961
Clearwater	Bagley	1902/1902	*		*	1903-56	1904-82	1902-76		
Cook	Grand Marais	1874/1901	*		*	1887-1952	1900-1975	1884-1982	1940-61	1960-61
Cottonwood	Windom	1857/1873	*		*	1871-1985	1872-1982	1883-1981		
Crow Wing	Brainerd	1857/1871	*		*	1871-1954	1884-1964	1878-1969	1960-71	
Dakota	Hastings	1849/1853	*		*	1854-1943	1866-69	1858-1966	1950-71	1880-1971
Dodge	Mantorville	1855/1855	1870-1945	1856-1925	1870-1945	1856-1955	1857-1982	1859-1982	1860-1931	1861-1971
Douglas	Alexandria	1858/1866	*		*	1867-1947	1868-1982	1867-1982	1867-1961	1867-1970
Faribault	Blue Earth	1855/1857	1863-1923	1857-1917	1870-1990	1850-1956	1863-1982	1858-1982		

COUNTY	COUNTY SEAT	YEAR COUNTY ESTABLISHED/ ORGANIZED[1]	VITAL RECORDS[2]			NATURALIZATION RECORDS[3]	PROBATE RECORDS		TAX RECORDS	
			Birth Records	Marriage Records	Death Records		Final Decrees	Will Books	Assessment Rolls	Tax Lists
Fillmore	Preston	1853/1853	*		*	1858-1955	1906-63	1858-1965		1901
Freeborn	Albert Lea	1855/1857	*		*	1853-1956	1870-1977	1857-1974		
Goodhue	Red Wing	1853/1854				1843-1951	1854-1983	1860-1982	1860-1961	1857, 1871-1961
Grant	Elbow Lake	1868/1883	*		*	1883-1943	1874-1972	1884-1955		
Hennepin	Minneapolis	1852/1852	*		*	1853-1942			1861-1900, 1951-70	1860-1961, 1980-81
Houston	Caledonia	1854/1854	*		*	1854-1943	1870-1982	1856-1982	1854-56	1861-1971
Hubbard	Park Rapids	1883/1887	*		*	1885-1955			1930-61	
Isanti	Cambridge	1857/1871	*		*	1871-1944	1875-1969	1875-1973	1869-1951	1865, 1867-68
Itasca	Grand Rapids	1849/1891	*		*	1891-1974	1891-1935, 1961-82	1898-1935		
Jackson	Jackson	1857/1870	*		*	1870-1953	1868-1982	1880-1982		
Kanabec	Mora	1858/1881	*		*	1867-1945	1888-1982	1885-1982	1859-1971	
Kandiyohi	Willmar	1858/1871	*		1946-80	1868-1954	1867-1982	1889-1982		
Kittson	Hallock	1878/1881	*			1881-1955	1882-1981	1882-1982	1879-1921	1879-1921
Koochiching	International Falls	1906/1906	*		*	1907-82				
Lac qui Parle	Madison	1871/1878	*		*	1867-1946	1874-1980	1876-1980		
Lake	Two Harbors	1856/1891				1884-1952	1888-1982	1890-1971		
Lake of the Woods	Baudette	1922/1922				1923-54	1924-82	1923-82	1930-81	1930-81
Le Sueur	Le Center	1853/1853				1862-1944	1855-1971	1918-74	1884-1961	1862-1971
Lincoln	Ivanhoe	1873/1881	*			1878-1951	1881-1983	1885-1982	1930-51	1930-51
Lyon	Marshall	1868/1875	*		*	1873-1956	1883-1982	1884-1982	1872-82, 1950-61	1873-98, 1941-70
Mahnomen	Mahnomen	1906/1906	*		*	1908-52	1907-82	1907-82		1940-71
Marshall	Warren	1879/1881				1853-1967				
Martin	Fairmont	1857/1857	1867-1940	1862-1952	1870-1992	1850s-1954	1866-1982	1869-1980		

COUNTY	COUNTY SEAT	YEAR COUNTY ESTABLISHED/ORGANIZED[1]	VITAL RECORDS[2]			NATURALIZATION RECORDS[3]	PROBATE RECORDS		TAX RECORDS	
			Birth Records	Marriage Records	Death Records		Final Decrees	Will Books	Assessment Rolls	Tax Lists
McLeod	Glencoe	1856/1856	*		*	1865-1953	1879-1982	1864-1980	1857-78, 1898-1971	1861-1971
Meeker	Litchfield	1856/1858	*		*	1858-1945	1857-1982	1864-1978		
Mille Lacs	Milaca	1857/1866	*		*	1861-1945	1875-1982	1882-1982	1864-1971	
Morrison	Little Falls	1856/1856	*		*	1856-1954	1885-1982	1875-1982		
Mower	Austin	1855/1856	1869-1945	1865-1952	1870-1993	1853-1955	1856-1971	1857-1970	1930-61	
Murray	Slayton	1857/1879	*		*	1856-1954	1873-1980	1875-1980		
Nicollet	St. Peter	1853/1853	*		*	1860-1956	1856-1976	1858-1960		1857-1961
Nobles	Worthington	1857/1873	*		*	1872-1959	1873-1982	1880-1982		
Norman	Ada	1881/1881	*		*	1882-1949			1882-1961	1882-1971
Olmsted	Rochester	1855/1855	1870-1999[4]	1855-1984[5]	1870-2000	1856-1957	1855-1964	1855-1964	1892-1971[6]	1890-1951[7]
Otter Tail	Fergus Falls	1858/1870	*		*	1870-1929	1872-1983	1875-1983		
Pennington	Thief River Falls	1910/1910	*		*	1911-77	1911-82	1911-82		
Pine	Pine City	1856/1871	*		*	1868-1958	1872-1948	1872-1942	1874-1981	1880-1970
Pipestone	Pipestone	1857/1881				1879-1954	1892-1982	1882-1982	1879-1971	1879-1971
Polk	Crookston	1858/1879	*		*	1870-1957	1968-82	1882-1982		
Pope	Glenwood	1862/1868	*		*	1866-1954	1867-1982	1872-1982		
Ramsey	St. Paul **	1849/1849	*		*	1849-1931	1897-1972	1849-87		1893-1901[8]
Red Lake	Red Lake Falls	1896/1896	*		*	1873-1943	1897-1972	1897-1972		
Redwood	Redwood Falls	1862/1868	*		*	1866-1948	1879-1982	1898-1981	1940-61	1868-1971
Renville	Olivia	1855/1868	*		*	1868-1946	1866-1980	1873-1976		
Rice	Faribault	1853/1855		1865-66	*	1856-1957	1856-1981	1857-1980	1858-1961	1860-1961
Rock	Luverne	1857/1874	*		*	1871-1957	1877-1984	1879-1984		

COUNTY	COUNTY SEAT	YEAR COUNTY ESTABLISHED/ ORGANIZED[1]	VITAL RECORDS[2]			NATURALIZATION RECORDS[3]	PROBATE RECORDS		TAX RECORDS	
			Birth Records	Marriage Records	Death Records		Final Decrees	Will Books	Assessment Rolls	Tax Lists
Roseau	Roseau	1894/1894	*		*	1885-1955	1894-1981	1897-1981	1895-1961	
St. Louis	Duluth	1856/1858	*		*	1867-1955			1940-61	
Scott	Shakopee	1853/1853	*		*	1853-1929	1856-1968	1857-1970	1864-1971	
Sherburne	Elk River	1856/1862		[9]	[9]	1864-1942	1855-1976	1865-99, 1957-59[10]	1859-1931	1860-1971
Sibley	Gaylord	1853/1854	*		*	1855-1945	1863-1982	1857-1982	1863-1951	
Stearns	St. Cloud	1855/1855	*		*	1852-1954	1865-1982	1864-1982	1855-1961	
Steele	Owatonna	1855/1856	1860-1950[11]	1856-1952	1870-1993	1853-1954	1867-1984	1858-1984	1859-1931	
Stevens	Morris	1862/1872				1872-1945	1877-1982	1928-81		
Swift	Benson	1870/1875	*		*	1849-1943	1873-1982	1881-1982		
Todd	Long Prairie	1855/1873	*		*	1868-1948	1869-1977	1872-1975		
Traverse	Wheaton	1862/1881	*		*	1881-1945	1884-1982	1882-1979		
Wabasha	Wabasha	1849/1856	*		*	1850-1942	1857-1974	1856-1974	1951-70	1859-1971
Wadena	Wadena	1858/1881	1880-1930	1873-1955	1880-1994	1873-1947				
Waseca	Waseca	1857/1857	1870-1983	1857-1982[12]	1870-1982[13]	1846-1966	1858-1978	1858-1979	1930-41	1862-64, 1930-41
Washington	Stillwater	1849/1849	1867-1987	1849-1952	1870-1994	1847-1944	1877-1965	1849-1965	1856-1951	1861-1960
Watonwan	St. James	1860/1871	*		*	1867-1945	1870-1977	1895-1981		
Wilkin	Breckenridge	1868/1873	*		*	1884-1945	1886-1974	1887-1982		
Winona	Winona	1854/1854	*		*	1854-1956	1872-1971	1857-1971	1940-61	1878-87[14]
Wright	Buffalo	1855/1855	*		*	1861-1944	1857-1982	1866-1982		
Yellow Medicine	Granite Falls	1871/1874	*		*	1850-1956	1874-1985	1882-1985		

INDEX

This book was designed and set in type by Will Powers at the Minnesota Historical Society Press. The type is Whitman, designed by Kent Lew. This book was printed at Maple Press, York, Pennsylvania.